500 COMPUTING TIPS
for TRAINERS

500 Tips from Kogan Page

500 COMPUTING TIPS
for TRAINERS

Steve McDowell and Phil Race

KOGAN
PAGE

London • Sterling (USA)

First published in 1998

Kogan Page Limited
120 Pentonville Road
London N1 9JN, UK
and
Stylus Publishing Inc.
22883 Quicksilver Drive
Sterling, VA 20166, USA

© Steve McDowell and Phil Race

British Library Cataloguing in Publication Data

A CIP record for this book is available from the British Library.

ISBN 0 7494 2675 6

Typeset by Jo Brereton, Primary Focus, Haslington, Cheshire
Printed and bound in the UK by Biddles Ltd, Guildford and King's Lynn

Contents

Introduction

We have written this book for trainers and, through them, for their trainees. In particular, this book is written for you if you use computers to support or to deliver your training, or if you already train in the broad field of information and communications technologies. We have particularly targeted our suggestions towards you if you are presently taking your first steps into particular aspects of the use of technology to support your training. We hope, however, that if you are a trainer with considerable experience in some of the uses of technology, you may find extra wrinkles among our suggestions that you can apply straightaway, and also that we may whet your appetite towards taking further steps to exploit some of the benefits which computers and technology can deliver both to you and to your trainees.

Trainers now work in a world that is experiencing dramatic and unprecedented change on at least two counts: the *amount* of information has expanded at an unprecedented rate; and the *availability* of information to anyone with a computer hooked up to the Internet exists in a way that was unimagined only a decade or two ago. Therefore, as trainers our role has changed far from merely filtering and transmitting information to our trainees, just as their needs have changed from merely acquiring and applying information, to developing their skills and competences. We, and our trainees, need to become developed as information processors rather than storehouses, and information and communications technologies are among the most powerful tools to help us all to do so. In particular, we need to help our trainees to become autonomous learners in the world of information technology and computers, so that they can continue to keep pace with developments throughout their careers and lives, long after they have completed our training programmes.

We have aimed to build this book out of practical, manageable suggestions and written in straightforward plain English! Each section of this book contains at least ten such suggestions. No doubt these will include ideas that you have already discovered for yourself and put into your own practice, or exceeded. We hope, however, that among our suggestions will be ones that will not yet have occurred to you, and which can save you time and energy, and provide you with short cuts to making effective use of computers in your own training.

It does not seem long ago that the principal resources used by most trainers comprised of overhead projectors, flipcharts, markerboards and face-to-face interaction. Many aspects of training technique were addressed by a previous volume in this series (*500 Tips for Trainers*, Phil Race and Brenda Smith, Kogan Page, 1995). Now, most trainers find themselves involved in using computers in one way or another, whether to prepare handouts and learning materials for

1

trainees, or as a means of delivering training presentations. In this book, we have mostly addressed areas not touched on in the previous volume, and particularly the use of computers in training.

The overlaps between the various applications in training of computers and information and communications technologies are widespread, and it proved quite difficult to separate the contents of this book into a logical clustering. We hope, therefore, that you will scan the contents pages and the book itself, in case the suggestions that may prove most useful to you are not in the part of the book where you might have expected them to be.

We have arranged the content of the book in six unequal chapters. Chapter 1: 'Helping Trainees to Learn' ranges wide, offering suggestions about the use of learning outcomes, then exploring various ways of helping your trainees familiarize themselves with keyboards and computers. You may well find yourself in the position of selecting or purchasing print-based or computer-based learning resource materials for your trainees, and we offer some questions against which you can interrogate both the learning quality and the content relevance of such materials. The same questions can, of course, be used to interrogate computer-based training resources which you may already have designed, or which you may plan to create. We offer suggestions in this chapter about making good use of a range of media to support both your training and your trainees' learning.

Chapter 2 is much shorter and more specific, focusing on computer-managed presentations. Many training venues are now equipped with computers and projection equipment, making it possible to carry in only a disk bearing your slides, rather than a wad of transparencies for the overhead projector. However, it takes a lot of courage (maybe foolhardiness!) to leave the transparencies behind when assembling your gear for a training session. In this chapter, we also look at the learning side of the equation, and explore ways of ensuring that trainees don't just go to sleep when you dim the lights for a computer-managed presentation!

Chapter 3 is on training *about* computers. We offer some basic suggestions about helping trainees to learn about computers in general, and word processing, spreadsheets, databases and computer programming. We suggest that even if your training content has nothing to do with computers, you might find it worth scanning this chapter, not least to help you to know a little more about how such things work, and perhaps to pick up the odd useful tip or short cut on using such applications as word processors or spreadsheets.

Chapter 4 is written for *you*! We have called it 'Reducing your Stress Levels', and it is particularly devoted to advice on ways of coping with some of the most common disasters (technology ones and human ones!), and suggestions about how to minimize the worry of travelling to distant parts of the country or the world with your training roadshow. Most of this advice is hard won from our own disasters!

Chapter 5 concentrates on e-mail, computer conferencing and the use of the Internet, which may be regarded as the principal manifestations of information and communications technologies in training. We have written our suggestions without assuming that you have any prior knowledge or experience of these technologies, and we hope that if you are already well into them, you will skip the suggestions that you already practise, and find useful ones that you may not have thought about.

Chapter 6 is about assessment. You may or may not be involved in formally assessing or examining trainees' performance, but if you are, we hope that this chapter will give you some pointers as to how you may use technology to make the process more efficient for you, and a greater learning experience for your trainees. The chapter ends with some tips on using computers to gather and analyze feedback *from* trainees, so completing the quality loop in training.

We started our own work as trainers using blackboards, whiteboards, overhead projectors and flipcharts. We still use these media, hopefully for things that they remain good for. We have found, however, that using computers and communication technologies has enriched our experience as trainers, and brought new dimensions and depth to the learning experiences of our trainees. We wish you well in your efforts to harness the versatility and power of technology in your own training.

Steve McDowell
Phil Race

October 1998

3

Chapter 1 Helping Trainees to Learn

Much of this book is about helping your trainees to learn effectively. In our first chapter, we have grouped together a range of sections which relate to effective learning as strongly as to effective training.

We start by asking some questions about why computers and information and communications technologies may be used in training. You might find it useful (and encouraging) to compare your own reasons for using such technologies with some of those we propose. We move on to some suggestions about expressing intended learning outcomes for your trainees. It is useful to think of these outcomes in connection with any training elements, and to use such thinking to inform your choice of training method and training materials.

Most effective learning happens when we *do* things rather than listen to others talking about them, and getting into computers is no exception to this. Our next sets of suggestions are about helping trainees to get started on using computers and keyboards. We also include some suggestions about the differences in keyboards, and conventions of punctuation, dates and times across the world. It is handy to know of these differences if you travel to train in foreign parts, or if your learners are likely to include some trainees from abroad.

We continue this chapter with some suggestions about selecting training materials, particularly those which you may plan to use with your trainees. We begin with some suggestions about choosing print-based materials, with particular regard to the quality of the learning that they are intended to deliver, then move on to some tips about making sure that the content is as relevant as possible to your intended training outcomes. This leads into some more specific suggestions about choosing computer-based learning materials.

Our next set of suggestions starts a dimension which will be a recurring theme in different parts of this book: using computers to give feedback to trainees.

We continue this chapter by looking in turn at some of the media which can play their parts in training: video, audiotape and multimedia learning packages. It is important to look at familiar and unfamiliar media from the point of view of how they can best help trainees to learn, and this is the stance we have taken throughout our suggestions.

We end this chapter by offering a range of suggestions about how computers can be used to help trainees to work together. This discussion leads into ways of keeping trainees working together even when they are separated in distant parts of the country or world, and brings in the uses of e-mail and computer conferencing, both of which are explored in more detail later in the book.

We feel that it is particularly important to make sure that, when using technology to support or deliver training, we do not allow ourselves to be carried away by our enthusiasm for any particular aspect of technology, and the running theme throughout this chapter is the quality and efficiency of the trainees' learning.

1

Why use computers and ICT in training?

Gone are the days when almost all training was done using the human voice, handouts, blackboards, markerboards and even overhead projectors. More trainers than ever are busily extending their repertoire so that they can keep up with the ICT (Information and Communications Technologies) revolution. There are many reasons for this, some better than others. You may like to start by seeing which reasons apply most to you (and adding any further reasons that appeal to you!).

1   **Because everyone else is doing IT!** That, of course, is not a new reason for changing one's practice. There are some good reasons for following the herd; you may be regarded as being old fashioned if you don't. However, don't follow everything that the herd does, …lemmings!

2   **Because you want to impress your trainees.** This is a natural enough reason for using computers and IT. However, if most trainers are doing it, you will need to find other and better ways to make the impression you want, unless you decide to use ICT *really well*. That is what this book is about, so you're heading in the right direction already.

3   **Because you want to impress your client.** This one is a rather risky reason. Your client may be impressed at the range of technology you require to carry out your training. Alternatively, your client may regard all this as a bit of a nuisance, and seek a trainer who can cover the same ground without all the fuss.

4   **Because you like playing with all the new-fangled gadgets you can lay your hands on.** This is a good reason, but just for you. After all, you may as well try to make your job as enjoyable as possible. The danger is that you may get carried away with the technology, and this could have bad effects on what your trainees actually manage to learn during your sessions.

5   **Because your boss has told you to get familiar with computers and such like.** This is a good reason, but mainly because you'll get the sack if you don't do it! However, help is at hand. In this book we hope we can make your venture into the world of computers in training a pleasant and productive one, and that you will end up liking it all as well as being good at it.

6   **Because you want to bring as much variety and interest as possible into your training sessions.** This is a very good reason. Holding trainees' attention is a crucial part of the job of any trainer. Concentration spans are short, but when there are plenty of different stimuli, concentration can be maintained much more effectively.

7   **Because your training *needs* the use of ICT.** This is a much better reason than most of the others in this list. You will already have good answers for exactly why you need each kind of equipment that you require, and your answers will relate directly to the intended learning outcomes associated with your training programme.

8   **Because your trainees need to experience things that they could not experience without you using computers.** This is a good reason. It also may imply that your trainees themselves will be doing something with the technology as part of your training session.

9   **Because your training is *about* ICT or computers.** This is a fine reason, of course. Although it is possible to conduct some kinds of training about things by just talking about them rather than using them, it is much more usual to want to match the training medium to the message for at least some of the time.

10   **Because you're already good at it.** It's always good when trainers do things that they are good at. If you're good at it, you'll probably enjoy doing it, and that will mean that some of your enthusiasm will pass over to your trainees, who will no doubt learn quite a lot more from you than if you were bored.

11   **Because you've got better reasons than we have thought of!** Well, who are we to argue with that?

2

Expressing intended learning outcomes

Just because you are using computers in your training, or indeed training about computer-related matters, does not mean that you should underestimate the usefulness of working out your intended learning outcomes and communicating them clearly to your trainees. Learning outcomes are being given increasing attention throughout training and education provision. There are various alternative names used for intended learning outcomes. These include objectives, goals, targets and competence statements (along with evidence indicators, performance criteria and range statements in formalized competence frameworks, such as those used by National Vocational Qualifications in the UK). Whatever we call them, it is important that they are useful to our trainees. The following suggestions will help you to get your trainees to make the most of learning outcomes.

1   **Remember that some of the language may be quite alien to your trainees.** If they've not already been mouse-trained, some may find the whole prospect of learning about computers quite daunting. Work out what your trainees should be able to do by the end of your training session, keeping in mind that some may be struggling.

2   **Find out whether similar learning outcomes have already been laid down.** The syllabus content of many education and training courses has been expressed in terms of learning outcomes, for example, in colleges which teach similar subjects. It can be useful to scan through a range of different interpretations of the learning outcomes associated with the subject matter you are handling.

3   **Express your outcomes in a user-friendly way.** Don't use wording like 'the expected learning outcomes of this session are that the trainee will be able to...'. It's much better to bring the word 'you' into your learning outcomes. For example, 'by the end of this morning, you'll be better able to do...', is much more involving for your trainees.

4   **Don't be limited by a prescribed training programme.** If you're starting from an existing formal specification of learning outcomes, translate it into user-friendly language for your trainees. As long as the net result is that your trainees gain the same competences and skills as were indicated in the formal specification, it does not matter if you express your learning outcomes in a much more friendly way. You can show your trainees the formal version of the intended outcomes *after* their learning has been successful, when they won't be put off so much by formal language.

5   **Don't use words like 'know' or 'understand' in your learning outcomes.** The problem with these words is that they mean different things to different people. It is difficult for people to tell whether or not they really understand something. The only way of measuring understanding is to find out what people can *do* with their understanding, so you might as well recognize this from the start, and express your learning outcomes in terms of the things your trainees will be able to do by the end of your session.

6   **Start with some relatively straightforward learning outcomes.** If the very first learning outcome that your trainees see is frightening, they are likely to be put off right from the start. Leave the tricky ones towards the end of the list, and perhaps don't reveal these until you know your trainees' performance well enough to judge whether they will accept them without being scared off.

7   **Remember that some of your trainees are likely to have *already* achieved some of your intended outcomes.** When introducing the intended learning outcomes, give credit for existing experience, and confirm that it is useful if some members of the group already have some experience and expertise that they can share with others.

8   **Be ready for the question 'why?'** It is only natural for trainees to want to know why a particular learning outcome is being addressed. Be prepared to illustrate each outcome with some words about the purpose of including it.

9   **Be ready for the reaction 'so what?'** When trainees still can't see the point of a learning outcome, they are likely to need some further explanation before they will be ready to take it seriously. Work out your answers to 'what's in this for me?' When trainees can see the short-term and long-term benefits of gaining a particular skill or competence, they are much more likely to try to achieve it.

10   **Make sure that the learning outcomes, as expressed, cover any assessment that trainees may be heading towards.** The whole point of learning outcomes is letting learners know exactly what it is that they should become able to do. If your trainees achieve all of your learning outcomes, they should automatically be in a position to demonstrate their achievement if their learning is to be measured. What's more, they should *know* that achieving the outcomes equates to success in assessment, so increasing their confidence when taking assessments.

3

Bringing trainees round to learning from a machine

Some trainees take to computers like ducks to water. Other trainees, however, are likely to believe that they need a human being to train them and that they can't learn from mere machines. The following suggestions may help you to win them over, so that they are more receptive to letting computers train them, too.

1 **Remind them that there's always a human brain behind the machine.** When necessary, explain to trainees that the computer is merely a vehicle for storing human expertise, and that it's not actually the computer that will be planning what they should learn.

2 **Tell them that the computer may be better than you are!** In other words, the expertise that will have gone into the computer-designed training packages is likely to be broader than that of any one person. The people who put together good quality training packages are normally very experienced in their field, and are likely to be expert trainers in their own right.

3 **Explain that working with computers is a transferable skill.** Gaining confidence and competence with computers is likely to spill over into future careers and lives, and will make your trainees more easily updated and retrained as further advances are made in their fields. Also, young people at school are increasingly highly mouse-trained, and many of your trainees may welcome the chance to keep up with their own children!

4 **Try to convince your trainees that learning from computers can be great fun.** Once they are over any fear that they will break the equipment, or that the computer will 'think' that they are silly, most people actually take pleasure in getting a computer to work for them.

5   **Remind your trainees of the comfort of making mistakes in privacy.**
When trainees get tasks or exercises wrong, in computer-based training only the computer knows – and computers don't mind! Therefore, it is much better to learn from one's mistakes using a computer than when human beings can see each and every slip.

6   **Point out that when using computers, your trainees don't have to waste time on things they already know.** In face-to-face training sessions, the whole group is often held up until someone catches up. With computers, anyone who already knows something can press on to something more demanding, without having to wait for anyone to catch up. Computer-aided training can allow trainees to work at their own individual pace.

7   **Computers don't mind the plea: 'run that by me again'.** Some things are not learnt properly first time around. It's not always convenient (or possible) to ask a human trainer to go once more through something that a trainee might find difficult, but a computer will go through it as many times as it takes to get the message firmly home.

8   **Remind your trainees that they learn most things by having a go at them.** When they learn-by-doing using a machine, they're being supported every step of the way, and most computer-based packages are highly interactive, and force trainees into making decisions, working things out, selecting the best answers to questions from a range of alternatives, and so on. This means that these aspects of their learning can be much more focused and efficient than in a group training situation.

9   **Suggest that human trainers are there for more important roles.** While trainees can learn things from machines, human beings are better at helping to measure and evaluate their learning, and explaining in other ways any parts which the computer was unable to teach them.

10   **Remind them that they don't have to work alone with computers.** While it may be intended that the computer-based training materials are for individual use and independent learning, it can be very useful for clusters of trainees to explore together a training package. This allows them to compare notes on what they find out, and to learn from each other and explain things to each other. This can be a useful first step before setting out to work through a package in depth, independently.

4

Helping trainees to learn-by-doing using computers

Learning happens by practice and trial and error. Learning happens by having a go. Not much learning happens when trainees simply watch an expert doing something. They are not then in a good position to do it for themselves. The following suggestions should help you to make your trainees' learning more productive and more enjoyable.

1 **Plan your training session around things that your trainees will actually do.** This is more important than simply trying to get together all the things that you might wish to tell them or show them. Map out the tasks that your trainees will do during a session, rather than simply mapping out the structure of the content that you intend them to cover.

2 **Share your intention to get trainees learning-by-doing.** Tell them how much more they will learn by having a go with computers (or anything else) than they would if they sat just listening to you talking about them. When trainees can see the point of doing practical tasks, even when they don't feel that they know enough to get started on them, they become more receptive to the idea of jumping in at the deep end (with plenty of lifebelts and floats around them).

3 **Remind your trainees that they're not going to break the computer.** Trainees who haven't used computers before are often afraid of damaging them, knowing that they are expensive pieces of equipment. They're extremely *unlikely* to damage them unless they are moving them physically.

4 **Tell your trainees about the benefits of learning-by-doing.** It helps when they know that this is the best way that they are going to make sense of the things that they are learning. It is useful to move their expectations away from simply listening to you explain things to them.

5   **Plan to let your trainees learn from their mistakes.** This is one of the best ways to learn most things, when mistakes can be made in a safe environment, and with help available for anyone who does not understand why a mistake happened.

6   **Remind your trainees that computers don't care about mistakes!** They may give error messages when instructed wrongly, but a computer does not get angry or frustrated, even when the same mistake is made several times in succession (unlike typical human reactions!).

7   **Make good use of anticipated mistakes.** Think of all the things that are known to be the most common problems with the subject matter you are handling, and set up learning-by-doing situations which will precipitate these likely errors. Let your trainees know that this is your intention, so that they themselves can be looking out for the errors and trying to avoid them.

8   **Build in practice and repetition.** For the most important things that your trainees will learn-by-doing, make sure that they consolidate their learning by repeating the steps involved two or three times during the training session. Structure these repeats differently, so that they don't get bored by the repetition.

9   **Remind your trainees that speed comes with practice.** They sometimes feel that their efforts are unbearably slow, especially if they see an expert like you gliding effortlessly through long sequences of steps at great speed. Let them see how much faster they do a task the third time through than on the first attempt.

10   **Get your trainees to talk each other through the steps that they have done.** This helps them to take on board consciously the sequences that they followed; putting it into words deepens their understanding of what they have done.

5

Getting trainees used to working with mice and keys

Becoming good at using computers, like most other things, is best learnt by doing it. The following suggestions may help you to make the processes of gaining skill with keyboards and mice more enjoyable and efficient for your trainees.

1   **Encourage your trainees to learn to touchtype.** They may not have time to do this during your training sessions, but if they really want to do it, there are good computer-aided training packages for just such a purpose. Explain that if they use computers a great deal, it is perfectly possible for them to become much faster at keyboarding than they may be at handwriting. Also explain that using the correct fingers for the right letters makes keyboarding easier in the long run, even though it has to be learnt in the first place.

2   **Remind your trainees that in most computer operations, not all of the keys need to be used.** The most important keys tend to be the 'enter' key (for commands), the letter keys for text entry, and the number keys for number entry or calculations. The function keys may be much more rarely used, especially when first starting to use computers.

3   **Make the most of 'undo' facilities in software.** In many word processing packages, for example, it is possible to 'undo' a series of keyboard entries. This can be particularly useful when trainees can't remember exactly what they actually did, but know that something has gone wrong. They can also try using the 're do' command, to find out, step-by-step, what they may have done when something went wrong.

4   **Consider the possibility of having at least one machine where plastic covers or stick-on labels obscure some or all of the letters on the keyboard.** This is one of the techniques used to help people to develop

touchtyping skills. Tell trainees who are using such machines not to look at their fingers at all, but to watch the letters on the screen as they type. Remind them that it does not matter if they type incorrect letters; they can always delete them and try again until they get what they are trying to get on the screen.

5   **Give your trainees computer-based exercises which require them to enter words or numbers from the keyboard.** Many computer-based training packages, and also computer-managed assessment programmes, require trainees to use text entry and number entry for their answers for at least some of the interactive elements.

6   **Help your trainees to become mouse-trained.** The best way for them to do this is simply to work through computer-based packages which require quite a lot of mouse work, such as using drop down menus, double clicking icons, and so on. Explain that it's a bit like learning to drive a car. While there are various kinds of mouse (including roller balls, trackpads and various other ways of manipulating the position of the cursor on the screen), once competence has been gained using one system, different systems are relatively easy to learn.

7   **Suggest to your trainees that they may benefit from varying the sensitivity of the mouse.** When they get really competent with a mouse, they are likely to prefer using fast speeds, but using slow speeds can help them to gain confidence on the way.

8   **Get trainees to experiment with the size and shape of the on-screen cursor.** The biggest source of anxiety, when learning to use a mouse, tends to be associated with 'losing' the cursor on the screen. Altering the colour and size of the cursor, to make it easier to spot, takes away much of this anxiety.

9   **Get your trainees to do some exercises using just the cursor keys on the keyboard.** These can usually do all the cursor movements that are normally done using a mouse, but are usually much slower and more cumbersome. Trainees are then more likely to appreciate the benefits of getting themselves mouse-trained.

10 **Choose some exercises that develop mouse skills.** It can be productive to get your trainees to play with a 'painting' programme, both to draw shapes and objects using the mouse, and to select and fill different areas of their drawings. People who have hang ups about their artistic skills often find that they exceed their own expectations when trying to draw using a completely new medium.

6

Language, visuals and numbers: international dimensions

The suggestions in this set may apply to you if you are likely to travel to different countries to run training programmes, or could involve your work with trainees from abroad who may find unexpected differences when they use computers here. Keyboards are not always what they seem to be. You may already have discovered this, but you still may need to alert your trainees to some of the wrinkles. You may work with trainees from several different countries, and it could be useful to be aware of some of the other keyboard possibilities which may be familiar to them. Furthermore, if you yourself train abroad, there may be some surprises in store for you; perhaps there are one or two points below that *you* have not yet discovered.

1   **There are many more characters available on the computer than there are on your keyboard.** If you want to type other characters, you may be able to use the menu bar in your application to insert characters or symbols. This option usually shows you a table and you can select the character you want from this.

2   **Set up 'shortcuts' for symbols that you use frequently.** You can set up a combination of key presses that will give you a symbol quickly. These usually involve using the 'Ctrl' or 'Alt' keys, together with one of the main keys on the keyboard. It is useful to pass on to your trainees examples of shortcuts which you find useful, and to encourage them to experiment with their own.

3   **Some typefaces have a wide range of different characters.** If you can't find a character that you want in the typeface you have been using, try other typefaces. Many computer systems have typefaces that contain

special symbols which you can use. The most common of these typefaces is called 'Symbol'. Help your trainees to practise finding any special characters they are likely to need in their own work.

4   **Make sure that other computers you wish to use have the correct typefaces.** If you produce a document using a special typeface, the symbols will look correct on your computer. If you view the same document on a computer that doesn't have that typeface, the computer will not display the symbols correctly and they may not appear at all. Point out to your trainees the sorts of problems that this may cause if they use computers from a different country.

5   **You can buy special typefaces for producing extra characters.** If the characters you want are not available on your computer, you may be able to buy an extra typeface which has them. As discussed above, this typeface will need to be on all computers that are to use your document. Explain the possibilities to trainees, but remind them that the chances of them actually *needing* unusual characters in their everyday work with computers or word processors is likely to be quite low.

6   **'Foreign' keyboards may have letters in different places.** This can lead to difficulties when you try to type. On some keyboards the differences are fairly small, but on others they are fundamental. If trainees from abroad seem to be having particular difficulties with the computers they use on your courses, it is worth finding out from them more about the particular differences they notice, so that you can build up your personal store of advice that you can offer to future trainees.

7   **Operating systems can be in other languages.** It can be a bit of a shock to start-up a computer and see all the menu items appear in a different language! If you are travelling, it is a good idea to try to familiarize yourself with appropriate computer terms in the language of the country you are going to visit. You might be expected to deliver training in English, but your interactions with the computer could be in a different language. Conversely, be patient with trainees from abroad who encounter an operating system in English for the first time.

8   **Make sure that you know how to set software to handle numbers correctly.** In some countries, numbers are represented differently to the way it is done here. You may need to change currency symbols, the number of decimal points displayed and the use of commas to show thousands and millions. You may, therefore, need to point out local conventions to trainees from abroad.

9   **Dates and times may be displayed differently.** Find out what is done in
     your destination country and how to set these correctly. Share with trainees
     from abroad the local conventions and preferences for showing or printing
     dates and times on documents.

10   **Check up on the use of punctuation marks.** These vary throughout the
     world, so make sure you are familiar with local practice in any country
     you are visiting, and let trainees from abroad know about your own local
     conventions. Make sure any notes you produce use these correctly and, if
     possible, ask a native of the country to check them for you.

7

Choosing print-based learning materials

Successful training is not all computer-based. Even when using computer-based training materials, it is likely that you will wish to use at least some print-based learning resources to support your trainees' learning. The next two sets of suggestions aim to help you to select effective and appropriate print-based learning resource materials for your trainees to work with. One of the problems with commercially available training materials is that some look good but just don't work, and others work well, but don't look attractive. Much published material falls between these two positions. What really matters is that the materials enable your trainees to learn successfully, but acceptable standards of appearance and style remain on the agenda. The following checklist may be a useful start when reviewing existing published materials, while exploring the possibility of adopting them or adapting them for your own trainees. Interrogate the materials on the following aspects of learning quality. Although these suggestions have been designed with print-based learning resources in mind, most of them extend to the decisions you may need to make about the learning quality of computer-based resource materials.

1   **Look first at the intended learning outcomes.** If these are well expressed, and in language that your trainees will be able to understand easily, the materials are off to a good start in your interrogation. It is also desirable that the learning outcomes are written in a personal, involving way, so that your trainees will feel that the materials are directly suitable for them.

2   **Check how interactive the materials are.** There should be learning-by-doing opportunities throughout the materials. Check whether the tasks and exercises are pitched at an appropriate level, so that they could give your trainees useful practice and the chance to learn from anticipated mistakes.

3   **Check how well the materials give feedback on trainees' efforts with them.** Look particularly at the responses printed in the materials to tasks or questions. These should be considerably more than simply answers to the questions. Your trainees should be able to find out not only whether their own attempts at the questions were successful or not, but should also be able to find out easily from the responses what might have gone wrong with their own attempts when unsuccessful.

4   **Check the standards.** The standards to which the learning outcomes will be delivered should be most clearly evident from the levels of tasks in the materials. In particular, if tutor-marked assignment questions are included in the materials, see whether they are pitched at an appropriate level for your trainees, and decide whether you may indeed use them as they stand.

5   **Think about the tone and style of the materials.** Most training materials work better when the tone and style is relatively personal and informal. The materials should be involving, with trainees addressed as 'you', and when appropriate the authors talking to trainees as 'I'. Check, however, that the tone won't be found patronizing by your trainees. This is not necessarily the same as whether *you* may find the tone or style too informal – remember that you are not *learning* from the materials.

6   **Think about the ownership issues.** For example, if the materials are designed for trainees to write all over them, filling in answers to questions, entering calculations, sketching diagrams, and so on, trainees are likely to get a high degree of ownership of their learning from the materials. If the materials are more like textbooks, this ownership may be reduced.

7   **Think ahead to what you may wish to add to the materials.** For example, when materials don't yet contain sufficient tasks and self-assessment questions, or when feedback responses are not yet self-sufficient enough for your trainees, you may well be able to bridge the gap by adding questions and responses of your own. This can be well worth doing if there are other aspects of the materials that make them particularly attractive as a starting point for your own fine tuning.

8   **Look at the layout and structure of the materials.** For trainees to trust them, the materials should look professional and credible. They should be able to find their way easily backwards as well as forwards through the materials. There should be good signposting, showing how each section of the materials fits in to the whole, and linking the intended training outcomes to the tasks and activities in the materials.

9   **See whether you can get feedback on how well the materials actually work.** Check whether there are other organizations already using the materials, and try to find out their views on how well the materials are found to work in practice. Reputable sources of published training materials will normally be only too pleased to provide details of major clients.

10   **Check the costs involved.** There are different ways of 'adopting' training materials. These range from purchasing copies in the numbers you require for your own trainees, to acquiring a site licence to reproduce your own copies. If you are dealing with a minority specialist option, the economics will probably favour buying copies directly. Bulk discounts may be available for significant purchases, and it can be worth buying in supplies to last for more than one 'run' of the materials, but this should only be considered when you are really certain that these are the materials that you want to use.

8

Choosing the most relevant learning materials

In the previous set of suggestions we looked at some questions with which to interrogate the *learning* quality of published training materials. Next, we explore some further important questions aiming to help you to establish the degree of relevance of the *content* of the materials to your own training programmes. Many of these suggestions apply equally to decisions you may need to make about print-based or computer-based learning materials.

1   **Check carefully the match between the published learning outcomes and those of your own training programme.** It is normal to expect some differences. Some of your own training outcomes may be absent from the published materials. The materials may at times go well beyond your own training outcomes. It is important to establish what fraction of the published materials will be directly relevant to your own training programme. If it is less than half, this is normally a signal to continue searching elsewhere.

2   **Check that the published materials are compatible with other parts of your trainees' studies.** For example, check that they use subject specific conventions or approaches that will be familiar to your own trainees.

3   **Seek out reviews of the training materials.** Just as with textbooks, reviews can help you to make decisions about which to adopt and which to reject; reviews of training materials can be useful indicators of their quality. Reviews tend to concentrate more on the subject matter than on the ways that the materials actually deliver successful training, and are therefore useful in the context of establishing relevance.

4   **Decide whether the materials are sufficiently up to date.** A quick way to do this is to look for references to 'further reading', or tasks briefing trainees to make use of other reference books or articles on the topics covered. You will normally know of the most respected source materials, and any recent developments which should be encompassed within the training materials, or referred to from them.

5   **Check that any resources that the materials depend upon are available.** For example, if the training materials are written with one or more set textbooks or articles to be used alongside them, make sure that these materials are still available. Even important set texts go out of print, often between editions, and the next edition may not lend itself to the particular tasks for which it was referred to from the training materials.

6   **Check the relevance of the tasks in the materials.** Compare these with the sorts of tasks you would set trainees on your own courses. Watch particularly for tasks which could be considered too basic, or 'missing the point' of important elements of learning. Also, look out for tasks which may be too advanced, and which may stop your trainees in their tracks.

7   **Estimate the expected time which trainees may need to spend using the materials.** There are often indications of this built in to training materials, but you may need to work out upper and lower limits that would reasonably relate to your own least able and most able trainees. Match these timescales to the overall duration (or equivalent duration) of your training programme, and the relative importance of the topics addressed by the materials. For example, if a published workbook is expected to take the average trainee 12 hours to work through, but the topic concerned is only one tenth of your 60-hour equivalent module, you may need to look for a more concise package covering the same ground.

8   **Check that you can live with the ways the materials address important topics.** This includes equal opportunities approaches. For example, check how the materials portray male/female roles in the content of case studies and illustrations. Don't get into the 'not invented here syndrome'. If you really don't like the way the materials handle an important concept, you are probably well advised to look for other materials. Any distrust or reservations you have about training materials may be quite infectious, and your trainees may quickly pick up doubts about the materials and lose their confidence to learn from them.

9   **Work out how much you may need to add to the materials.** It is quite normal for published materials not to cover everything that you would if you were designing them yourself. It is relatively easy to bridge small gaps, by designing handouts or small workbooks to address them.

10   **Work out how much you might wish to delete!** You don't want your trainees to waste their time or energy by doing things in published materials which are not connected to the learning outcomes of their own programmes, or which are not involved in their own assessment in some way. It is perfectly feasible to brief your trainees on such lines as 'Don't do anything with Section 9 unless you want to just for your own interest; it's not on your agenda'. To decide which published materials you may wish to adopt, make sure that there is not too much in this category.

9

Choosing computer-aided packages

Computer-based packages are widely used in training, and play a valuable part in open learning programmes, and indeed have largely been developed for the open learning market. As open or flexible learning pathways become used more widely within training provision, the range of computer-based learning resources continues to grow rapidly. There may well exist computer-based packages which will be helpful to your own trainees, and it could be more cost effective to purchase these and adopt them as they stand (or adapt them) than to design new materials of your own. The following suggestions may provide you with help in selecting computer-aided learning packages for your trainees.

1   **Remember that it's harder to get a good idea of the effectiveness of computer-based materials than for paper-based ones.** This is not least because it is not possible to flick through the whole of a computer-based package in the same way as is possible with a printed package. It can be quite hard to get a feel for the overall shape of the learning that is intended to accompany a computer-based package.

2   **Choose your packages carefully.** The best computer-based learning packages are not always those which look most attractive, nor are they necessarily the most expensive ones. The best indicator of a good package is evidence that they enable learning to be successful. Where possible, try them out on trainees before committing yourself to purchasing them. Alternatively, ask the supplier or manufacturer for details of clients who have already used the packages, and check that the packages really deliver what you need.

3   **Prepare your own checklist to interrogate computer-based materials.**
    Decide the questions that you need to ask about each possible package,
    before committing yourself to purchase. Questions could include:

- Are the materials supplied with workbook elements?

- Do trainees themselves *need* these elements?

- Can support materials be freely photocopied?

- What is the standard of the equipment needed to run the packages
  effectively?

- What level of technical support and backup will be required?

- Does the software include individual trainee progress monitoring and
  tracking?

- Do the materials make good use of pre-test and post-test features?

- Can the materials run effectively on a network?

- Are there licensing implications if you wish to run the package on more
  than one machine?

- Can you afford multiple copies if the materials are multimedia, single
  access packages?

4   **Try to establish the pedigree of the software.** Some computer-based
    packages have been thoroughly tested and developed, and have been
    updated and revised several times since their launch. Such packages
    normally give some details of the history of their development. Beware
    of packages, however well presented, that have been published or
    disseminated without real trialling.

5   **Find out about packages from colleagues in other institutions.** Use your
    contacts. Ask them about packages they know of, which work well and
    really help trainees to learn. Also ask them about packages that they don't
    rate highly, and about the factors that led them to this conclusion.

6   **Try before you buy.** Computer-aided learning packages can be quite
    expensive, especially if you need to purchase a site licence to use them on
    a series of networked computer terminals, or to issue trainees with their
    own copies on floppy disk. If you're considering buying a particular
    package, try to get a sample of your trainees to evaluate it for you. Their
    experience of using it is even more valuable than your own, as only they
    can tell whether they are learning effectively from it.

7   **Look at how the medium is used to enhance learning.** If the material does no more than to present on screen what could have been presented equally well on paper, it is probably not worth investigating further. The medium should do something that helps learning, such as enabling trainees to engage in interaction that they may have skipped if the same tasks or questions were set in print.

8   **Get familiar with the package, before letting your trainees loose with it.** There is a learning curve to be ascended with most computer-based packages, and it is best if *you* go up this ahead of your trainees. They will need help on how to make best use of the package, as well as on what they are supposed to be learning from it. Find out what it feels like to use the package. By far the best way to do this is to work through the package yourself, even if you already know the subject that it covers. Find out what trainees will *do* as they use the package, and check whether the tasks and activities are really relevant to your trainees, and pitched at an appropriate level for them.

9   **Check the intended learning outcomes of the computer-based package.** The best packages state the intended learning outcomes clearly within the first few screens of information. Alternatively, the intended outcomes may be spelled out in supporting documentation which comes with the package itself. The main danger is that such packages address a wider range of intended outcomes than are needed by your trainees, and that they may become distracted and end up learning things that they don't need to, possibly interfering with their assessment performance.

10   **If necessary, rephrase the learning outcomes associated with the package.** It may be useful to tell your trainees exactly what the learning outcomes mean in the context of their particular studies. This will help them to concentrate on the most important things in the package.

11   **Think about access to equipment and software.** It can be prohibitively expensive to give or loan each trainee both the software and the hardware needed. However, if the package is an important part of their overall programme, ways need to be found to maximize their opportunity to work with it. Some packages come with licence arrangements to use the package with a given number of trainees, either allowing multiple copies to be made or the package to be used over a network. Ensure that the software is protected in order to prevent unauthorized copying or unlicensed use on more than one machine.

12   **Think how trainees will retain important ideas from the package, after they have used it.** Make sure that there is supporting documentation or workbook materials, as these will help trainees to summarize and remember the important things they gain while using computer-based packages. Where such resources don't already exist, you should consider the benefits of making a workbook or an interactive handout, so that trainees working through the package write down things (or record them) at important stages in their learning.

13   **Ensure that learning-by-doing is appropriate and relevant.** Most computer-based packages contain a considerable amount of learning-by-doing, particularly decision-making, choosing options, and entering responses to structured questions. Some of the tasks may not be entirely relevant to the intended learning outcomes of your open learning programme, and you may need to devise briefing details to help trainees to see exactly what they should be taking seriously as they work through the package.

14   **Check that trainees will get adequate feedback on their work with the package.** Much of this feedback may be already built in to the package as it stands. However, you may need to think about further ways of keeping track of whether your trainees are getting what they should from their use of the package. It can be worth adding appropriate, short elements to tutor-marked assignments, so that there is a way of finding out whether particular trainees are missing vital things they should have picked up from the package. One of the main strengths of computer-based learning packages is that trainees can be given instant feedback every time they select an option in a multiple-choice question, or key in a word or phrase, and so on. The feedback should be much more than just the correct answer to the question or task. Trainees who get things wrong need to find out from the programme *why* their answer or response was wrong, and exactly *what* was wrong about it.

15   **Check how long the package should take.** The time spent by trainees should be reflected in the learning payoff they derive from their studies with the package and this, in turn, should relate to the proportion of the overall assessment framework that is linked to the topics covered by the package. Many computer-based learning packages come with indications of the expected timescales that are involved in using them, but it is well worth finding out how long typical trainees actually take. Some computer-based packages can make this easier for you by logging the amount of time individuals spend working through them.

16   **Think ahead to assessment.** Work out what will be assessed, relating directly to the learning that is to be done using the computer-based materials. Express this as assessment criteria, and check how these link to the intended learning outcomes. Make sure that trainees, before working through the computer-based materials, know *what* will be assessed, *when* it will be assessed, and *how* it will be assessed.

17   **Explore software that keeps track of trainees' progress.** Many computer-based materials can be used to track individual trainees' progress through them. This can involve pre-testing and post-testing, and storing the data on the computer system, as well as monitoring and recording the time taken by each trainee to work through each part of the package. Such data can be invaluable for discovering the main problems that trainees may be experiencing with the topic, and with the package itself.

18   **Seek feedback from your trainees.** Ask them what aspects of the package they found most valuable and most important. Also, ask them what, if anything, went wrong in their own work with the package. Look in the feedback you obtain for anything that throws light on particular categories of trainees finding difficulties with learning from the package (for example, speakers of other languages, or mature trainees, or people who are uncomfortable with new technologies). Where possible, find alternative ways of addressing important learning outcomes for those trainees who have particular problems with the computer-delivered materials.

10

Using computers to give feedback to trainees

Feedback is a vital step in successful learning. Human beings can get bored when giving the same feedback repeatedly to different trainees; computers don't have this problem! In the suggestions which follow, we look at computer-generated feedback, where you program the feedback messages you wish trainees to receive in anticipated circumstances, such as replying to options in multiple-choice questions. We explore the use of computer-delivered feedback in more detail later in this book, where your individual comments are e-mailed directly to individual trainees, or put up on a computer conference where all the trainees can see such comments. The following suggestions may help you to use computer-generated feedback to make your training more effective for your trainees, and more enjoyable for yourself.

1   **Look for those occasions where you frequently need to give the same feedback message to different trainees.** Work out exactly what the gist of your feedback message is on such occasions, and consider whether it will be worthwhile packaging up this feedback so that trainees can get the same help from a computer instead of from you.

2   **Listen to yourself giving live feedback to trainees after they have attempted a task.** It can be worth tape recording some examples of the way you talk to fellow human beings. The little 'asides' that you slip in to make sure they understand you are very important, and it's worth incorporating such asides in the feedback you get the computer to give them.

3   **Devise a task relating to the planned feedback message.** Normally, the feedback will be reserved for those trainees who don't get the task right first time. Check out with live trainees that the planned feedback is self-sufficient, and that they don't need any further explanation from you in person to get the task right next time.

4   **Don't forget to provide feedback to trainees who get the task *right* first time.** It is just as important to give positive feedback for successful work, as it is to give helpful feedback when trainees encounter problems. Remind them exactly *what* they got right, in case it was a lucky accident.

5   **Let trainees who get things right know about some of the things that might have gone wrong.** Learning from mistakes is useful, and people who don't make any mistakes can miss out on some valuable learning. Trainees are often quite hooked on finding out more about what they *might* have done wrong, even when they got it all right.

6   **Be sympathetic to trainees who get it wrong.** When you programme feedback into a computer-based learning package, it is important that your trainees feel that the computer is treating them like human beings. Don't include blunt messages such as, 'Wrong!', or 'Wrong yet again!' It is better to come across almost apologetically, with feedback messages starting perhaps as, 'Sorry, but this doesn't work out in practice...'.

7   **Remind trainees about *what* they get wrong.** It is important that mistakes can be linked firmly to the task that brought them about. The danger is that when your trainees read your feedback messages, as programmed into the computer system, they may have forgotten exactly what they were trying to do when things went wrong.

8   **Try to devise feedback which explains *why* trainees may have got something wrong.** It isn't enough just to know *what* was wrong. Whenever you can, devise feedback messages about mistakes along the lines, 'For this to have happened, you may have been thinking that..., but in fact it's like this...'.

9   **Road test your feedback messages with small groups of trainees.** Ask them if they can think of any better ways of getting the feedback message across. Get them to put into words what *they* might have said to someone sitting next to them who attempted the same task, and got it wrong. If their words are better than your original ones, steal theirs!

10   **Explore the possibilities of using e-mail for 'later' feedback.** When you know how well (or badly) trainees have tackled a computer-based exercise, you may be able to give them feedback through the system of networked computers. This means that only the trainees concerned see each feedback message, and they have the comfort of privacy in which to read the feedback and think about it, without you seeing their expression or body language.

11

Using video for training

Video recordings are widely used in many forms of teaching and training, and already play a valuable role in helping to show trainees things that they would not be in a position to explore on their own. You may already use video extracts to support your own training, or give trainees video materials from which to learn selected elements of their programme. With computer-based training, there are often video sequences embedded in multimedia programmes. However, the act of watching material on a television-screen is not one of the most powerful ways through which trainees actually learn, unless the video extracts are carefully planned into their learning programme. The following suggestions may help you to assist your trainees to make the most of video.

1   **Decide what the intended training outcomes directly associated with the video extracts will be.** It is important that any video extracts are not just seen as an optional extra by your trainees. The best way to prevent this from happening is to tell them exactly what they are intended to gain from each extract of video material.

2   **Decide why video is the best medium for your purposes.** Ask yourself 'what is this video extract doing that could not be done just in print?' Video extracts can be invaluable for showing all sorts of things that trainees could not experience directly, as well as for conveying all of the subtleties that go with body language, facial expression, tone of voice and interpersonal interactions, skills and techniques.

3   **Decide *how* the video material is planned to help your trainees to learn.** Is it primarily intended to whet their appetites and stimulate their motivation? Is it designed to help them to make sense of some important ideas or concepts which are hard to learn without seeing things? Is it designed to give them useful briefings about things they themselves are intended to do after watching the material?

4   **Consider whether your trainees will need their own copies of the video.** If the trainees are expected to watch the video a number of times, and at their own choices of points during their training, you may need to issue them with personal copies, or make them available on loan. Alternatively, you may be able to arrange that the materials can be viewed on demand in a resources centre. If so, make sure that there are mechanisms enabling trainees to book a time slot when they can see the video material.

5   **Decide what your trainees will take away after watching the video.** One of the dangers with video extracts is the 'now you see it, then it's gone' situation. If the video is serving important purposes for your trainees, they will need to have something more permanent to remind them of what they learnt from it. Remember, even if they have their own copies of the video material, they are unlikely to find time to revise from it directly. It is important that they have some other kind of summary of what they are expected to remember from it.

6   **Work out what (if anything) will be assessed.** If the video is just 'icing on the cake' and there is nothing arising from the video material that will be directly involved in any form of assessment, tell your trainees that this is the case. When things they derive from using the video elements *are* involved in their assessment, explain this to them, to help them to give the video materials appropriate attention.

7   **Use short extracts at a time.** People are conditioned to watch quite long episodes of television, but to do so in a relatively passive way. Make sure that your trainees approach video extracts in a different way than that which they normally use for watching television. It is better to split up a 30-minute video into half a dozen or so separate episodes if there are several different things you wish your trainees to get out of the material. Some video materials have timings encoded on to the video tape.

8   **Set the agenda for your trainees before each episode of video.** This can be done on the video extracts themselves, or in accompanying printed materials. Either way, ensure that your trainees are set up with questions in their minds to which the video extracts will provide answers.

9   **Consider giving your trainees things to do while they view the video extracts.** You could brief them to note down particular observations, or to make particular decisions, or to extract and record specific facts or figures as they watch the video extracts.

10 **Consider asking your trainees to do things after they've watched each extract.** This can help them to consolidate what they have gained from watching the extracts. It can also prompt them to have a further look at any extract where they may have slipped into passive viewing mode and missed important points.

11 **Don't underestimate the importance of printed support materials.** To make the most of video elements, trainees need something in another medium to remind them about what they should be getting out of the video, and where it fits into the overall picture of their learning. Video recordings often work best when supported by a printed workbook, into which trainees write their observations and their interpretations of what they see. Their learning from such workbooks can be reviewed by looking again at them, even without looking again at the recording.

12

Using audiotapes for training

Audiotape is so commonplace and cheap that its potential in training contexts is easily overlooked. In subject disciplines such as music, where sound is all important, the use of audiotapes as a training medium is already well developed. In multimedia packages, sound and images are often combined to good effect, yet audiotape can sometimes play a similar role at much less cost. The use of audiotapes to support training can be extended to many disciplines. The following suggestions may remind you about the pros and cons of learning through hearing when trainees use audio visual learning programmes, and may also inspire you to put simple audiotape to good use to support your trainees.

1   **Have good reasons for using audiotapes.** Always be in a position to explain to your trainees *why* an audiotape is being used alongside their other training resource materials. Share with them information on what they should be getting out of using the audiotape.

2   **Most trainees have access to audiotape.** Many trainees have portable cassette players, and may use these when travelling on public transport, or jogging, or driving and in all sorts of circumstances. When elements of training packages are available as audiotapes, there is the possibility that you will extend their training to times when they would not otherwise be attempting to study.

3   **Label audiotapes informatively.** People who listen to tapes tend to accumulate lots of them, and it is easy for audiocassettes accompanying learning programmes to get lost amid those used for entertainment.

4   **Keep audiotape extracts short and sharp.** When there are specific intentions about what trainees should get out of listening to audiotapes, extracts should normally last for a few minutes rather than quarters of an hour! It is worth starting each extract with a recorded 'name' such as, 'Extract 3, to go with Section 1, Part 2', and to have the same voice reminding trainees that when they have reached the 'End of extract 3, going with Section 1, Part 2', and so on.

5   **Use audiotape where tone of voice is important.** It can be particularly useful for trainees to hear messages, where the emphasis that you place on key words or phrases helps them to make sense of material which would be harder to interpret from a printed page or from a computer screen.

6   **Sound can help trainees into subject-related jargon.** When there is new terminology, for example, it can be hard to tell how to pronounce a word just by seeing it in print, and it can be humiliating for trainees to find only when talking to a trainer that they have got their pronunciation wrong! Audiotapes can introduce the vocabulary of a subject to trainees.

7   **Use audiotapes to bring training to life.** Audiotapes can be invaluable for giving trainees the chance to hear people talking, discussing, debating, arguing, persuading, counselling, criticizing, and can capture and pass on to them many experiences and processes which would be difficult to capture in print.

8   **Clarify exactly when a recorded episode should be used.** If you are using audiotape alongside printed materials, it can be useful to have a visual 'flag' to indicate to your trainees when they should listen to a recorded extract.

9   **Turn trainees' listening into an active process.** Listening can all too easily be a passive process. Avoid this by setting your trainees things to think about before listening to a tape extract. Prime them with a few questions, so that they will be searching for the answers from what they hear.

10   **Consider using audiotape to give trainees feedback on their assignments.** It can be quicker to talk for a few minutes into a tape recorder, than to write all of your feedback down on your trainees' written assignments. The added intimacy of tone of voice can help you to deliver critical feedback in a more acceptable form. Trainees can also play the tape again and again, until they have understood each part of your recorded feedback. Always try to begin and end with something positive, just as you would do with written feedback.

11   **Combine audio and visual learning.** It can be useful to use audiotape to talk trainees through things that they are looking at in their resource materials. For example, complex diagrams or derivations in printed materials, or graphics, tables, spreadsheets shown on-screen in computer-based materials, can be brought to life by the sound of a human voice explaining what to look for in them.

13

Interrogating multimedia for training

Training packages can contain, or refer to, an increasing range of other sorts of material. We explored the use of videotapes in a separate set of suggestions, but the present set aims to alert you to the questions you should be asking yourself about *any* medium. This could range from CD-ROMs, the Internet, intranets, interactive videos, and anything which adds sounds, still pictures, moving images, graphics, to the experience of trainees working through training materials.

1   **How does the medium help trainees' motivation?** Ideally, any multimedia component should help trainees to want to learn from them. If there are too many steps to getting going with the multimedia elements, there is the danger that trainees can be put off and may be stopped in their tracks.

2   **Can the medium be used to provide some learning-by-doing?** Perhaps the biggest danger with some multimedia packages is that however sophisticated the media used, trainees may only be spectators rather than players. Where it is not possible to cause trainees to interact directly with the materials, it remains possible to get them to make decisions, answer questions, summarize conclusions and to write down these for later reference.

3   **Can the medium be used to give trainees feedback?** The danger is that the information presented using multimedia is often fixed, and cannot then respond to what trainees may be thinking about it, or to the problems or misunderstandings that may be in their minds. It is best to ensure that some self-assessment questions address directly any important information presented in multimedia formats, so that feedback responses can be designed for trainees to address such difficulties.

4   **How does the medium help trainees to make sense of things?** There are often excellent answers to this question. For example, sounds, pictures, moving images and colourful graphics can all play a useful part in helping trainees to get their heads around things with which they have been grappling.

5   **Why is this medium better than other, cheaper media?** For example, why is a computer-based package better than a print-based one? There are many good answers to this question. The best answers are when the medium chosen does something that just cannot be done by other media; for example, moving pictures showing body language and facial expression where such dimensions are crucially important for getting particular messages or attitudes across to trainees.

6   **How relevant will the medium-based element be to the overall training programme?** One of the dangers with media-based training is that too much 'nice-to-know' material may be involved, and not enough emphasis placed on 'need-to-know' material, and that trainees may not easily be able to distinguish between the two categories.

7   **How will the choice of medium affect trainees' opportunities to learn?** For example, will they only be able to study the particular elements concerned when they are sitting at a networked computer terminal, or when logged on to the Internet? Will this mean that they have frequently to stop learning until they can gain such access? Will there be alternative coverage of these elements of training for any trainees who have not got easy access to the medium, and can it be guaranteed that they will not end up disadvantaged?

8   **How easy will it be to edit and change the medium-based elements?** Training materials are never 'finished'. There are always adjustments and changes that are indicated from piloting, feedback from trainees, and from assessments measuring how well trainees actually succeeded in their learning. Some media are much easier to edit and change than others. Changing a CD-ROM or videodisk is a much more complex (and more expensive) business than changing a file in a computer-based package.

9   **What *other* media could have been used?** There is rarely just one way to package up a particular element of learning. It is useful to explore at least two or three alternative ways of using media to deliver each element of training, and then to make an informed decision about *why* a particular medium is chosen.

10   **How will trainees revise and consolidate what they have learnt from the medium?** What will they have to take away? Will they be able to make a structured summary of what they learnt while working with the medium, which will bring all the important points back to their minds when looking at it later?

14

Helping trainees to work together

Using computers is often thought of as a solitary activity. Many of us use PCs – personal computers – and this name suggests that they are meant for individual use. Computers can, however, be very useful for group activities. Group working can have many advantages, ranging from the interchange of ideas to providing social contact. It can also lead to problems as some groups do not perform well and some people do not thrive in group work situations. When the group is widely dispersed, it is even more important than usual that steps are taken to help groups to function properly. Working together at a distance may sound paradoxical, but sometimes it is easier to arrange group activities in this way. Because of computer communications, barriers of distance and timing can be lowered. In order for your trainees to participate, they will need e-mail facilities as a bare minimum. For even more effective communications, computer conferencing will be needed. We explore e-mail and computer conferencing in more detail in Chapter 5, but include below some pointers on how to use these to keep trainees working together. The following suggestions may help you to get groups to work together productively, whether as part of your training programmes, or using computer conferences at a distance.

1   **Think carefully about the number of people who should be in each group.** If groups are too small, the trainees may have to work too hard and they may not have all the skills needed for the task. If the groups are too large, they may be unwieldy and it might be difficult for decisions to be made. In large groups, there is a risk that skills can be duplicated so that some people are underutilized. When you decide on a size for each group, bear in mind that you might not have exactly the right number of trainees to divide up, so you will have to have a range of sizes in mind.

2   **Decide whether you will choose who is in which group or whether the trainees will organize themselves.** If you choose, you have more control over the whole process of group working. If the trainees organize themselves, they will feel more empowered and will be taking more responsibility for their work.

3   **Think about the task the groups will have to tackle and how it affects the composition of the 'ideal' group.** Some tasks require special skills and it may be necessary to distribute skill holders amongst the groups. These skills could be related to the task in hand, or they could be group skills such as leadership. Some thought may also need to be given to whether the groups need to be balanced so that they have a roughly equal chance of doing the task effectively.

4   **Carry out some group building tasks before the main group task starts.** If the groups are to work effectively from the beginning of a task, they must be functioning effectively as groups first. The members also need to be familiar with the computer conferencing system, if you are using one. Set up some minor tasks first so that the trainees can gain experience and the roles within the groups can be established.

5   **Develop group tasks that enable individuals to use their particular skills.** Your trainees may not all have learnt about the same computer skills, or some may be more proficient in some areas than others. Carefully chosen group tasks can involve real team work in distributing tasks amongst the group so that people can use their skills effectively.

6   **Use group tasks to help to distribute skills.** Someone who is particularly proficient in a skill can help other members of a group to improve their skills. This has an additional benefit of making the skilled person think hard about what they can do in order to show another person how to do it.

7   **Encourage negotiation skills in distributing tasks amongst group members.** When a group is given a task, people will have to take on different roles. Some of these roles may be unpopular; others may be everybody's first choice. Help the group to negotiate so that they all feel that they are performing a useful role and that the allocation of tasks is fair.

8   **Set group tasks that involve the group meeting new challenges.** When an individual is faced with a task that goes beyond their current knowledge, it is easy for them to feel overwhelmed by its difficulty. The dynamics of a group can help with this, as the interactions between group members will often lead to new avenues of thought which can find ways round blockages.

9   **Plan group activities that build on skills that have been developed elsewhere.** It is useful to use group work to help trainees to consolidate things they have already learnt, and to give them the chance to see how useful it can be to learn by explaining things to each other. This can save you time, too.

10 **Use group activities to help people to appreciate each other's work.** If trainees who work in different fields tackle work related problems together, it will also give them some appreciation of each other's work. This can help to develop team building that will continue when their computer training is over.

11 **Encourage computer communications between trainees as soon as possible.** In order to make effective use of computer communications, regular use is needed. If trainees can develop a culture of frequently checking e-mail and conferences, they will make very effective use of these media. If they only check occasionally, there will be a struggle to establish their effective use.

12 **Set some simple tasks early on.** You could pair trainees up and give them a simple task which requires them to exchange ideas. They could then produce a joint word processed report on what they have done. This would mean that they would need to communicate with each other and they could also need to exchange files attached to e-mail messages.

13 **Give everyone some practice at using computer conferencing.** If you plan to use computer conferencing to keep trainee group work going after a face-to-face course, or between elements of such a course, it is useful to use part of the course time to get everyone talking to each other electronically. Ideally, you will need a room with networked terminals for each trainee. It can be useful to start everyone off with a common interest topic, even one that has no relationship to your training programme, and allow your trainees to concentrate on the process of communicating with each other electronically, rather than thinking too hard about the content of their practice communications.

14 **Put out information by e-mail or in conferences to make people check for it.** Rather than sending out all the documents by mail, use computer communications for some of it. Warn your trainees that you are going to do this and keep doing it so that they continue to check their e-mail and conferences.

15 **Make sure some kind of backup is available.** If someone didn't receive a computer message because of technical problems, it could cause major problems for them. Some sort of safety net could be used: for example, you could send out a message to all trainees every week. Anybody who didn't receive the message would know to contact you so that you could try again or send a paper copy to them in the normal mail.

16 **You might need to consider geographical location when setting up groups.** If your trainees are widespread, there is no need to consider where they live and work. If some of them live or work near to each other, they could meet occasionally. This might help the group to work well, but it could also give them an unfair advantage over other groups who couldn't meet face to face.

17 **Make sure groups have ways of communicating apart from electronic means, such as computer conferencing or e-mail.** As with all technological systems, computer conferences can fail to work. It is very important that some backup communication system can be used. Ideally, group members would exchange telephone numbers, fax numbers and addresses. Check what rules your institution has about releasing personal details, however, as there are often controls on this.

18 **Set up private conferences for each group at an early stage.** Each group will need a conference where they can exchange messages that cannot be seen by members of the other groups. Set these up for them early in the process (or, better still, appoint a member of each group to do it). Make sure that the conferences contain suitable topics and remember to include a 'chat' area so that there is a suitable place for general conversation.

19 **Decide on your own access to group conferences.** The groups' conferences could be closed to you, so that you cannot read them and trainees can discuss any topic freely. This may help trainees to feel uninhibited about what they say in messages. Alternatively, you could have access to them so that you can monitor progress. Make sure that the trainees know what you have decided so that they can behave appropriately!

20 **Encourage trainees to take part in group activities regularly.** The group work will not only be taking place at a geographical distance, but also at different times. It is very important that all group members access their conference regularly, and that they leave messages to show that they are doing so.

21 **Include a group work topic in the main conference.** It will be very useful for members of different groups to have a common area where ideas and problems related to the group task can be discussed.

22 **Make use of any facilities software has for tracking who has done what.** Some packages (particularly word processors) have features that show who has written or revised different parts of a file. These enable some checking over who has done what they were supposed to.

23 **Make sure that somebody is in charge of the group.** It is easy for a group to encounter serious problems if there is no control over their activities. One person needs to take on the role of coordinating the whole group to make sure that all the tasks are progressing properly. When groups undertake several successive tasks, encourage the groups to decide who will coordinate their work on a rotating basis.

24 **Watch out for particular problems that can arise from computer use.** When groups are using computers, it is possible for out-of-date documents to become confused with current versions. If there is a failure of any kind, the consequences affect the whole group, so backups are particularly important. Somebody needs to be in charge of this area to make sure problems don't develop.

Chapter 2   Using Computers in Your Presentations

In our previous chapter, the emphasis was on trainees' learning. In this short chapter, we move on to one particular aspect of using computers in training, that of designing and using computer-managed presentations. The most common presentation manager we know of is Microsoft PowerPoint, but our suggestions should extend to any such computer-managed presentation format.

We start by posing some questions to make sure that you really want to start using computer-managed presentation packages for the right reasons. If you are already using such packages, we invite you to test your rationale against our questions.

Even the best designed presentations can be let down if the room layout is unsuitable, so we offer a checklist of suggestions that you can use next time you plan to use such a presentation. We follow with some don'ts for using presentation managers, mostly learnt from our own trial and error!

However well designed, and well presented a computer-aided presentation may be, it is important not to forget that the ultimate intention is that the audience should *learn* useful things from it. The remaining two sets of suggestions in this chapter aim to help you to make sure that computer-delivered presentations do not degenerate into a 'rest from thinking' for your trainees. In particular, the 'now you see it, now it's gone' issue applies to computer-managed presentations, but also extends to the use of all media where information is presented on a screen, whether in a training room, or on a monitor.

15

Deciding whether to use computers

There are several good reasons for using computers in presentations, and at least as many bad ones. The following points may help you to decide when you will use them, as a start towards making effective use of them in your training.

Some good reasons...

1   **Because you want to show your trainees about computers.** This is an obvious good reason for building computers into your presentation, but you may not always have the chance to do it. However, remember that trainees will not automatically become able to use computers themselves just by watching you use one. The best position is to use computers in your presentation to illustrate things that your trainees will very shortly be having a go at themselves.

2   **Because you want to whet their appetites.** Computer-aided presentations can help your trainees to *want* to become able to do the same sorts of things as you show to them. Don't, however, end up with the opposite result and frighten them away from experimenting for themselves.

3   **Because you want to make a good impression on your audience.** There is sometimes some truth in the view that 'the medium is the message', and people may think that if you are just using old-fashioned ways of giving presentations in your training that your message itself may be outdated. However, the quality of your use of the medium is just as important as choosing an up-to-date medium.

4   **Because you want to be able to edit your presentation easily and frequently.** Computer-generated presentations are very easy (and very inexpensive) to edit, even to restructure completely. It is much easier to

adjust a computer-delivered presentation after every experience of giving it, than it would be to prepare a new set of overhead transparencies each time.

5　**Because you want your handout material to relate directly to your presentation.** In PowerPoint presentations, for example, you can print off handout pages containing multiple slides. You can also annotate individual slides to make handouts with additional notes and background information. The strongest advantage of printing out your slides in handout materials is that your trainees then don't need to do menial tasks such as simply copying your slides into their own notes, but can do more active things such as writing their own notes on to their printouts of your slides.

6　**Because you want to show things that can't be shown using traditional methods.** For example, if you want to show your trainees pictures, moving images or graphics which would be difficult or impossible to illustrate using overhead transparencies, you can be fairly sure that you are justified in making your presentations computer-aided.

7　**Because you want to be able to have *all* of your training presentations available.** A single floppy disk can carry hundreds of slides of presentation material. If your training repertoire is wide and varied, it might be impossible to carry it all around with you on overheads or handouts. Carrying a few disks is much more feasible, and you can customize a new presentation from your repertoire quite easily, once you have had some practice at editing, and print off those handouts you need locally.

8　**Because you want your trainees to be able to have another look at your presentation later.** You can give trainees your computer-managed presentation on disk, to work through at a machine in the training room, or even on their own machine at home or at work. You can even e-mail a presentation to trainees at a distance.

Some bad reasons...

1　**Because everyone else seems to be using computer-aided presentations.** This may be a reason for making at least some of your presentation computer-aided, but it is worth thinking hard about whether computers provide the best medium for the exact purposes of each element of your presentations. It is better to mix and match, rather than to switch blindly to a different way of supporting your presentations.

2   **Because the equipment happens to be there.** Some training centres and venues lay on computer-delivered presentation systems as a matter of routine. It is still possible to use overhead projectors, markerboards and flipcharts, too! Sometimes, these may be pushed out of sight to make room for the computer and projector, but they are usually not far away.

16

Setting out your training room

A problem with using computers as training tools is that they are designed for interaction with one person, not a group. This means that it is very difficult for more than two or three people to see the same computer screen clearly. It is even more difficult for a few people to sit comfortably around a computer screen for any length of time. The following suggestions aim to help you set out your training room to minimize visibility problems.

1   **Position computers carefully to avoid reflections on the monitors.** If reflected light is shining on the screens of the computers, it can make it very hard and tiring to read the data. One person may be able to find a suitable position in order to avoid this problem, but it can be difficult for several people to see the data.

2   **Anti-glare screens can improve screen visibility.** You can reduce reflections on monitor screens by adding a special screen in front of the monitor. There are several types available, but if you want to use a screen to help with group work, check that it allows clear viewing from a range of angles. Some of these screens are even designed to restrict the viewing angles in order to improve security.

3   **Close blinds to reduce glare from outside light.** It can feel a bit claustrophobic to be in a room with no natural light, but you may need to close some or all of the blinds or curtains to help with glare problems. If some windows aren't contributing to this problem, don't cover them.

4   **Avoid using laptop screens for group viewing.** The screens in most laptop computers are small and not very bright. Even more importantly, they usually only allow viewing from straight in front, so they are not at all suitable for viewing by several people at the same time. If you want to use a laptop computer, check if you can connect it up to a full sized desktop monitor, or a projection system.

5   **Try to avoid the 'computers around the wall' layout.** Because it is the simplest way of routeing the cables of the computers, a common layout is to put all the computers around the walls. The trouble with this is that all you see, as a trainer, is the back of people's heads. This layout also makes it difficult for your trainees to look at you, or at anything else in the room.

6   **Make sure that all the cables are safe.** Make sure that cables aren't anywhere near people's feet to avoid any danger of them tripping over them. It is also easy for people to pull leads out of the back of computers with their feet, without realizing that they have done so.

7   **It may be possible to use a large computer monitor, mounted fairly high up.** It is possible to connect more than one monitor to a computer, if the right hardware is available. This means that you could work at a computer, looking at its screen, whilst your trainees see the same information on a large screen. Large computer monitors are expensive, but there are adaptors available which allow televisions to be used in this way. This is cheaper, but the quality of the image can be poor.

8   **Information can be displayed on several ordinary computer monitors simultaneously.** There are devices on sale which plug into a computer and several monitors to allow several people to see the information simultaneously. Using these requires some changes to the wiring of the computers in the room, so you will need to check if this is possible and if it would interfere with the normal operation of the computers.

9   **A computer network might be able to display the same information on several monitors at once.** If your computers are linked together in a network, this is a possibility worth checking. You will need to ask your network manager if this is possible and to ask for help in setting it up.

10   **Overhead projection 'tablets' are available.** These devices connect to a computer and duplicate its display on a transparent liquid crystal display. This can be put on an overhead projector and projected onto a screen. These devices can be expensive and you will need to make sure that outside light can be reduced to help make the projected display clear. It is usually even better if you can hook up the computer directly to a projection set-up, such as used for projecting videos. These normally give a brighter, and better focused display than liquid crystal tablets.

17

Some don'ts for presentation managers!

For many trainers, the most familiar presentation manager is Microsoft PowerPoint. Any presentation medium can be used well or badly. Computer-generated presentation managers are being used increasingly, instead of overhead projection and other simpler means of supporting presentations. The following suggestions should help you to avoid some of the most common pitfalls with presentation managers. Many of the suggestions are based on our own experiences of using PowerPoint in our work, and the feedback we have received from our trainees about it.

1   **Don't cause 'death by bullet point'!** Even though computer-aided presentation packages can introduce bullet points to slides in a variety of ways (fly from left, dissolve, and so on), bullet points can quickly become tiresome to an audience. It is worth having a good reason for building any slide step by step.

2   **Don't overdo the special effects.** You can program your whole presentation to build slide text either in a single way (for example, fly from left) or randomly. Doing the whole presentation in a single format becomes boring for your audience, but programming a random sequence of slide building tends to be irritating for you as the presenter, as you don't know what build sequence will be produced when you move to your next slide. Similarly, don't go overboard on the snazzy changes from one slide to the next. Presentation managers can move from one slide to the next in a variety of ways, which you can program for each separate change, or program all to be the same, or program to occur in random sequence. The random sequence can actually turn out to be quite irritating, especially if you are using successive slides to progressively build up a detailed picture, in which case you need to move from one to the next without any special effects.

3   **Don't use it just like an overhead projector substitute!** Simply transferring the contents of your overhead transparencies into a computer delivered presentation does not make full use of the medium. For a start, you are unlikely to get as much information into a single computer-projected slide as you might have done on an acetate sheet. Try to do *other* things with computer-aided presentations, for example, making good use of the possibilities of moving images, graphics and so on.

4   **Don't forget that it's not that bright!** Most computer-aided presentation packages rely on projection equipment that is not nearly as bright as a good overhead projector. This means that you may need to take particular care with room lighting, daylight from windows, and (worst of all) direct sunlight. If you use a liquid crystal display tablet, it isn't a good idea to place it on top of an ordinary overhead projector; you need a high powered one (1000 W or more) for reasonable visibility.

5   **Don't forget to check the focus before you start.** If you're using equipment you've not used before, don't go ahead with a PowerPoint presentation if the focus is not good. Some projection systems are fine for video projection, but turn out to be too fuzzy for computer-managed presentation projection. Modern systems have easy ways of adjusting the focus, but older systems may need to be set up in considerable detail before an acceptable image quality is produced, or may just not be capable of producing clear still images. If you can't get the image sharp, don't go ahead with your projection, but revert to other means such as overhead transparencies. Looking for any length of time at fuzzy images can give some members of your audience headaches, as their eyes try in vain to compensate for the fuzziness.

6   **Don't forget the conditions appropriate for human sleep!** Turning down the lights, sitting comfortably in the same place for more than a few minutes, and listening to the sound of your voice may be just the right conditions for your audience to drop off.

7   **Don't forget that sunlight moves.** If you're setting up a training room first thing in the morning, you may need to plan ahead for where any sunlight may be later in the day. Sunlight moves in opposite directions in different global hemispheres.

8   **Don't put too much on any slide.** We can still count on our fingers the number of computer-aided presentations we have seen where *all* of the slides were perfectly readable from the back of the room. It is better to have twice as many slides, rather than to cram lots of information on to each slide. It usually takes two or more slides to project the same amount of information that would have taken one overhead transparency.

9   **Don't put important text in the lower half of slides.** Unless all members of your audience have an uninterrupted view of the screen, people sitting at the back will tend to have to peer around their nearer neighbours to read any text at the bottom of the screen. Unlike overhead projection, you can't simply move a transparency up the platen to make the final points visible to people at the back.

10   **Don't use 'portrait' layout.** You will usually have the choice between landscape and portrait, so use landscape to make the most of the top part of the screen. You may already have found that the same applies to overhead transparencies.

11   **Don't import tables or text files.** The fact that you *can* import such files into a computer managed presentation package leads many into temptation. These are very often the slides which can't be read from the back (or even from the front). It is normally better to give trainees such information as handouts, rather than to try to show them it on-screen.

12   **Don't use the wrong colours.** Colours that look good on a computer screen don't always show up so well when they are projected. If most of your presentations will be in rooms with natural daylight, it is usually best to stick to dark colours for text, and light (or even white) backgrounds. If you know you're going to be working in a lecture theatre where you have full control of the lighting, you can then be more adventurous, and use light lettering against dark backgrounds (not forgetting that you may be lulling your audience when you turn down the lights).

13   **Don't use the same slide format for all of your slides.** Computer-managed presentation packages may allow you to switch your whole presentation into different preprepared styles, but the result can be that your slides all look too similar to have an optimum learning payoff for your viewers. Vary the layout, colours and backgrounds, so that each new slide makes its own impact.

14   **Don't leave a slide on when you've moved on to talk about something else.** It is better to switch the projection off, rather than to leave up information that people have already thought about. If you're within reach of the computer keyboard, pressing 'B' on some systems causes the display to go black, and pressing 'B' again brings the display back. This is far simpler and safer than switching the projector to standby, and risking having to wait for it to warm up again when you want to project your next slide. An alternative is to insert a 'black' slide, where you wish to stop your audience from looking at the screen. Don't, however, forget where you've placed these, and panic about where your display has gone!

15   **Don't talk to the screen!** With overhead projectors, it's easy to develop good habits, including looking at the transparency rather than at the screen, and avoiding turning your back on your audience. With projected images, you may have no alternative but to watch the screen, but you need to make sure that you talk to your audience. If you can arrange things so that you can look at a computer screen rather than the projection screen, the problem can be partly solved. However, in one of our cases at least, switching one's gaze between computer screens and audiences alternately may require frequent changes of one's spectacles, and this in itself can be irritating to an audience.

16   **Don't go backwards for too long!** If you need to return to a slide you showed much earlier, it is better to switch the display off, and find the slide you want without your audience seeing every step. The same applies to returning to your original place in your presentation.

17   **Don't neglect the things that computer managed presentations packages do, that overhead projectors don't.** For example, it is worth finding out how to use animated graphics, video clips, and colour photo images, to liven up your presentation, and to show your audience that you know how to do such things.

18   **Don't forget to rehearse your presentation.** With overhead transparencies you always know what is coming next; with presentation managers it is all too possible to forget. If *you* look surprised when your next slide appears, it does not do much for your credibility with your audience.

19   **Don't underestimate the potential of remote controls surprising you!** Many systems allow you to change slides with a remote control connected to your computer, or to the projection equipment. Pressing the wrong button on this can switch the system to something quite different (for example, video input), and can mean that you can find yourself unable to get back to your presentation without losing your cool. It is best to find out in advance which buttons *not* to press, and possibly to place some adhesive tape over them to reduce the possibility of pressing them.

20   **Don't forget to check your spelling.** PowerPoint, for example, can do this for you, but you have to instruct the software appropriately. Be careful not to let the software replace words automatically, or you will get some strange overheads if you are using unfamiliar words.

21   **Don't fail to get feedback on your presentation before you run it.** It is really useful to get someone else to watch your slides, and to ask about anything that isn't clear, or point out anything that could irritate an audience.

22 **Don't neglect to adjust and improve your slides.** It is so easy to alter a set of slides that there's no real excuse for not editing your presentation frequently until you have got it finely tuned. The most beneficial additions are often new slides inserted to address frequently asked questions in advance.

23 **Don't stop watching other people's technique.** This is one of the fastest ways of improving your own presentations. Look for things that work well for other people, and find out how the effects were achieved, then emulate them. More importantly, look for things that don't work, and make sure that you avoid them.

24 **Don't forget your overheads!** It is still useful to have at least some of your computer slides on traditional acetate. Machines can go down. More likely, you can still press the wrong button on a remote control, and switch your projector on to video or off altogether. At such times, it can seem lifesaving to be able to go to an overhead projector, at least temporarily.

18

Helping trainees to learn from computer-aided presentations

Computer-aided presentations are increasingly being used as part of training programmes. They often replace lectures, demonstrations or talks. However, as with lectures, the danger remains that trainees may not necessarily learn a lot, even from good presentations. The following suggestions may help you to encourage your trainees to make computer-aided presentations an active learning experience.

1   **Remember that people don't actually remember a great deal of what they see.** Keep your computer-aided presentations down to relatively small, self-contained episodes, and intersperse them with activities that involve your trainees in learning-by-doing, or other activities such as discussing, prioritizing, or summarizing.

2   **Get your trainees to formulate some questions before you start your computer-aided presentation.** For example, ask groups of trainees to decide what they want to find out about the topic you're going to cover, and to write down some questions that they hope will be covered. When they have already got questions in their minds, they are much more receptive to the answers when your presentation addresses the questions. You may, of course, need to make sure that all of their questions have indeed been answered at the end of your presentation, and spend a little extra time covering those questions that were not covered by your prepared presentation.

3   **Work out the objectives of each part of your computer-aided presentation.** Show these on-screen, and explain exactly *why* each objective is important or relevant to your trainees. Explain to them what *they* should expect to be able to do to show that they have achieved the objectives in due course. People are more receptive to information when they know what will be expected of them.

4   **Help your trainees to *make* notes.** This is much more productive than merely *taking* notes, such as when they copy down things they see on the screen, or write down verbatim things that you say. When you give your trainees copies of your computer-projected slides, you can encourage them to annotate their copies, adding in thoughts of their own and questions that arise in group discussion.

5   **Build tasks into your computer-aided presentation.** Get your trainees to *do* things with the information that is presented on-screen, rather than just watch it. Use your computer slides to pose questions and then answer them, rather than just present the answers alone. Get your trainees to work out which are the most important points from an on-screen list, or to work out the consequences of changing the conditions in a scenario.

6   **Include questions to trainees in your presentations.** For example, pose a question on-screen, then pick a trainee at random to try to answer it. Don't make the trainee too uncomfortable if an answer is not immediately forthcoming, however. When trainees become accustomed to being put in the position of having to try to answer a question at short notice, they naturally become more attentive, as no one likes to be found lacking an answer.

7   **Get trainees to make summary notes every now and then.** It can be worth pausing in the middle of a computer-aided presentation, and asking your trainees to write down the three most important things they think they should try to remember about what they have been watching.

8   **Review the objectives of your presentation as you approach the end of it.** This can be a useful way of reminding your trainees of the importance of the main points covered by the presentation, and can lead neatly in to the next stage of your training session, which may be to give them some practice at working towards achieving the objectives.

9   **Consider making your presentation available to trainees, to consult individually, after the group has seen it.** It is normally straightforward to install your presentation on a computer, where your trainees can have the chance to refresh their memories of it when they choose to. Alternatively, if your trainees have their own computers, or regular access to computer provision, you could consider giving them copies of your presentation on disk. You may be wise to make such copies 'read only', and have your name clearly as a footer on each slide, to prevent anyone from pirating your expertise.

10   **Seek feedback on your computer-aided presentation.** It is worth finding out from your trainees which aspects of your presentation really help them to understand the topic concerned. Also ask them what they found most enjoyable, and what they liked least about the presentation. If several trainees disliked the same aspect, it's usually well worth changing it. It is also useful to devise a quiz, short test or exercise to probe how effectively your trainees actually learnt things covered by your presentation. When several trainees are found to have a shared difficulty, it is usually a signal to try to adjust the relevant part of your presentation, often by inserting one or two further slides addressing the difficulties that you now know about.

19

Now you see it, now it's gone!

This is one of the most significant pitfalls of computer-aided presentations or demonstrations. Trainees may well understand something while they are watching you show it to them, but their understanding may slip away quite quickly when they can't see it any more. The following suggestions may help you to overcome the problem.

1   **You know it all already!** This is always the case when, as an experienced trainer, you have the problem of not being quite able to imagine not knowing the topic! With computer-aided presentations, the problem is in trying to work out which parts of your presentation are likely to go over trainees' heads first time through. Once you have identified the elements that you really want them to remember, you are in a much better position to take positive steps to help them to remember them.

2   **Be a trainee yourself for a while.** It can be really useful to sit in on someone else's computer-aided presentation, or to work through a computer-based training package on something that you don't know anything about, and then to look at what was memorable, and what was all too easily forgotten. This can inform the way you help your trainees to maximize their learning from your own presentations and materials.

3   **Plan for them to *do* something, fairly quickly.** Relatively little learning happens just by watching something passively. More significantly, trainees' expectations of what they should be learning are mostly based on what they are asked to do. Look carefully at which parts of your computer-delivered presentation lend themselves to be the basis for fairly immediate tasks for trainees, and make sure that your trainees know what they will soon be required to have a try at for themselves before they watch your presentation, so that they will do so more attentively.

4   **Design triggers, which will bring back trainees' memories of things they have seen.** This is quite easy to do in the case of PowerPoint slides, where you can provide trainees with handout pages to remind them both of the content of individual slides, and the sequence of the whole presentation.

5   **Stop and switch the presentation off every now and then.** Design tasks to get your trainees recalling and consolidating what they have just seen and heard. Think about short tasks that they can do in twos or threes where they are sitting, so that they can be reminded of the main things that you wish them to remember from the episode of presentation that they have just seen.

6   **Consider turning a presentation into a question and answer session.** You can brief trainees with the questions on-screen, then turn off the presentation while they try to work out (or guess) answers to the questions. When you resume the presentation, they will be more receptive to the answers that your presentation already contains, than if they had not been trying to answer the questions themselves for a while.

7   **Get trainees to annotate copies of what they see.** If you issue printouts of computer-presented slides, it can be useful to make many of the slides bullet point questions, and to encourage trainees to write summary answers to each question as you work through the presentation with them.

8   **Get trainees to *do* things with what they see.** For example, ask them to complete a pro forma while watching a video sequence or a software demonstration. Brief them in advance about the main things they should be watching out for, and the questions already on the pro forma. Stop the demonstration or video quite frequently, to give them time to make sense of what they have been seeing, and to record it in their own words on the pro forma.

9   **Use screen dumps to illustrate your handout materials.** This can be an effective way of helping trainees to recall important stages of demonstrations they have watched on-screen. Make sure that screen dumps are clearly legible – don't print them too small!

10   **Don't illustrate indiscriminately.** Each illustration in your handout materials should have a definite purpose. It is best if you can give your trainees something to *decide* each time they see an illustration in their handouts, so that they really look at the illustrations.

Chapter 3 Training about Computers

Much of this book is about using computers yourself, to help with your work as a trainer. The aim of this short chapter is to give you some ideas about training others in the use of computers. Even if you don't think you will ever do this, it is worth giving it a quick read as there may be some ideas here that could improve your own use of computers.

We start with some suggestions on training about computers in general, including a summary of useful advice to give to trainees who are new to using computers. You may even find one or two points that are helpful to you regarding your usage of computers.

Our next set of suggestions is about word processing. This is a particularly useful skill. Not only will it be useful for your trainees to develop this skill, but developing it yourself can save you a great deal of time and trouble when designing your own training resource materials, such as handouts, exercises and assessments.

Spreadsheets are often seen as rather frightening by those of us who are not yet familiar with them, but can save a great deal of effort when used in appropriate circumstances. Our suggestions on training about spreadsheets are intended only to be a basic introduction to the area, but enough to help your trainees (and yourself, if necessary) get into the learning-by-doing stage of developing mastery of them.

Creating a database is something that most computer users may not have ever done before. We include some suggestions for helping trainees, who need this skill, to get started. Finally, we include some tips on getting trainees started on computer programming. The number of people who actually *need* to develop computer programming skills is far less than the computer-user population, however, and it is important to make sure that your trainees actually need to develop programming skills before starting in this direction with them.

20

Training about computers in general

Computers are used for so many purposes that it is impossible for a trainer to know about them all. Additionally, the pace of change in the computing world is so fast that it is difficult to keep up. As a result, trainers will need to think clearly about what training they can offer and what needs to be bought elsewhere. At the very least, it should be possible to develop sufficient knowledge of computer basics and the use of the most common computer applications to meet the initial training needs of beginners. Similarly, trainees will usually only need to learn about specific areas of computing, so care needs to be taken over what to cover with them.

1   **Don't spend too much effort on the technical details of how the machines work.** Users need to know enough to operate the computer effectively, but a large amount of technical knowledge will only tend to confuse them. Familiarity with the use of disk drives is essential, and some idea of the role of Random Access Memory (RAM) might be useful. Only serious users need to know about buses, motherboards and pipeline cache modules.

2   **Familiarity with the operating system is very useful.** Beginners will need to feel confident about starting applications and moving their files about. Make sure they spend enough time on this at a fairly early stage and that they develop a good understanding of what they are doing.

3   **Point out the similarities between different applications.** The screen layout and menu bars of modern applications often conform to a standard system. Beginners will feel more confident when they recognize words and symbols that they have already learnt about when using another application.

4   **Encourage regular saving of files as a safety measure.** If your trainees develop the habit of saving their work frequently, they will have an extra safeguard against making mistakes. If something goes wrong, they can reload their work and try again.

5   **Keeping different versions of files can be helpful.** By using the 'Save As…' option and specifying a different file name, it is easy to keep old versions of a file. One of the old versions might be useful if things have gone badly wrong later on.

6   **It may be best for trainees to save files on floppy disks.** Training is often carried out in a training suite and the computers will be used for a range of courses. If files are saved on to the hard disk, others may erase them or the machine may not be available for the next session. If work is saved on to floppy disks, the work can be used on any suitable machine. Additionally, trainees may be able to take their floppy disk to a machine to do more work on the files between sessions.

7   **'Undo' facilities can be very helpful.** Many applications allow commands and typing to be undone. This can be a great help as it means mistakes can be corrected very quickly. Sometimes a series of operations can be undone and redone, allowing an easy review of what has happened.

8   **Encourage independence.** In the initial stages, your trainees will probably look to you for help all the time. Because computers are so complex, you will not know all the answers to everything and you won't always be there to help. Encourage your trainees to use other resources for help. These resources can include Help files, manuals, tutorial material and other trainees.

9   **Set up 'problem solving' groups.** If a few people are coping well with basic tasks and others are still struggling, you can set a small group a more advanced task. They can use all the resources available to find out how to do it and possibly run a small presentation on it for the others.

10   **Try to use real tasks that relate to people's jobs.** Initial tasks will have to be simple, but the training will seem more purposeful if trainees can relate their training to their jobs. Try to find exercises that will help to clarify the relationship and encourage trainees to bring problems from their work to you.

11   **Encourage trainees to help each other.** One of the best ways of crystallizing new knowledge is to explain it to somebody else. When trainees help each other, you can have very lively training sessions and you will have more time to help those in most need.

21

Training about word processing

Almost everybody can benefit from some knowledge and experience of word processing. The concept behind it is simpler than for any other computer application, so it is a good starting point. While basic word processor operation is simple, modern packages are capable of very sophisticated work and can produce complex documents. They can also be used for powerful operations, such as mail merges. Many word processors can even use a programming language to carry out frequently repeated, complex tasks. Word processing is also a very useful skill to have as it makes the production of high quality documents a possibility for anyone. Finally, many of the skills developed when learning how to word process are transferable to other computer applications.

1   **Explain different options for selecting text.** The mouse is very useful for selecting text; for example, to move, copy or delete it. Other techniques, such as double clicking, clicking in margins and dragging are very useful and less well known. They can make selecting and modifying text much faster.

2   **Show how text can be deleted accidentally.** A common problem that beginners have is that they select some text, then type something. The selected text is then replaced by what they have typed. This can be useful, but beginners often have trouble with work 'disappearing' because of this. Show them how this works and how to 'undo' it to reclaim their work.

3   **Showing non-printing characters can help people understand problems.** Most word processors allow you to show characters such as spaces and carriage returns that aren't printed and don't normally show on the screen. Making these visible can help beginners to understand why the computer is behaving the way that it is.

4   **Have samples of formatted text to show trainees how to produce high quality work.** It is very easy to select text and change its font or size, its alignment or its colour. This makes it easy to produce a range of styles, but help will be needed in order to avoid having too many effects and to produce clean looking pages.

5   **Develop familiarity with Cut, Copy and Paste.** By selecting text and then cutting it, copying it or pasting it into another place, documents can be modified easily. These techniques are also useful for entering text repeatedly. It is often possible to use keyboard commands for these functions and this can be faster than using the mouse to access menus.

6   **Encourage the use of headers and footers.** These add information automatically to all the pages in documents. The information can include page numbers and the date as well as any text of the user's choice.

7   **Show how numbering and bulleting can help clarify some documents.** It is easy to add numbers or bullets to lists. Paragraphs can even be numbered or bulleted automatically as they are typed, and it is possible to automatically label sub-sections.

8   **Make sure the tab key is used for indenting text.** Most fonts used on word processors are proportional. This means that if spaces are used to indent text, correct alignment may be impossible. Even if indenting looks correct on the screen, it may print out incorrectly. Show your trainees how to use tabs and how to set them to the spacing that they want.

9   **Explain how to use borders around paragraphs.** Borders are very good for separating sections of text. Show how they are created and how the lines can be modified and turned on and off.

10   **Raise awareness of the benefits and dangers of spell and grammar checkers.** Spell checkers are very useful for finding errors, but they have major limitations. They only check the words that are in their dictionary: they can't check for missing or wrong words. Grammar checkers can help with finding errors but they can also lead to a very restricted style of writing. Encourage their use, but insist on a final, careful reading of text to spot any errors that have slipped through.

11   **Give trainees some safe practice at global editing.** For example, give them a floppy disk with a word processed document file on it, and ask them to global edit selected words, such as 'was' to 'is', 'were' to 'are', 'double quotes' to 'single quotes', and so on. Also help them to improve the layout of the document, for example, by changing all multiple spaces to single spaces between words and sentences. It can also be very useful to global edit changing each 'manual line break' to a space, for example when inserting some scanned-in text into an existing document.

12   **Help trainees to make good use of the 'Find... Replace' command.** This can be useful when they remember making a mistake, but have forgotten where it was in the document. It is also useful to dump something unusual (xxx, &&, ppp, and so on) at points in a long document that they may want to return to quickly, and just use the 'Find' command to return immediately to such points. It is best that these anomalous oddities are such that they would be picked up by the spell checker facilities later, if they happened to be forgotten!)

13   **Show how 'AutoCorrect' can be used to enter repeated terms quickly.** AutoCorrect is designed to correct frequent typing errors (such as 'teh' instead of 'the'). Users can enter their own corrections and this can be used to enter long words quickly. As an example, imagine that you are typing the word 'substantiate' frequently in a document. If you tell AutoCorrect to replace s with substantiate, every time you type s, the full word will appear. You can even do this for complete phrases, such as 'ict' becoming 'information and communications technologies'. Magic! It is important, of course, to make sure that you don't end up with a nonsense phrase creeping into ordinary language. The 'Undo' facility can be used to undo single instances of an AutoCorrect modification, such as if you really want say 'ict'.

14   **Don't go into unnecessary complications.** For example, most word processing packages can perform 'Mail Merge' operations, suitable for adding names and address details on letters to a list of different people. However, the number of word processor users who actually *use* this facility tends to be much lower than the people who have met it on a training programme!

15   **Encourage people to use word processing to help them with their jobs.** Word processing programs contain many powerful features. These include mail merging, inserting pictures and tables and using 'foreign' characters, but there are many others. If trainees are aware of these, they can identify which of them would be useful in their work and learn how to use them.

22

Training about spreadsheets

Spreadsheets do for numbers what word processors do for text. Anybody who has to deal with numbers could find a basic knowledge of spreadsheets useful. They are particularly effective when a task has to be repeated regularly: weekly summaries of figures, for example. The basic functions of spreadsheets are simple: a lot can be done with basic arithmetical operations. There are also a large number of built in functions available on modern spreadsheets, which make them very powerful. If these aren't advanced enough, there is often a complete programming language, which makes the package capable of performing very complex tasks.

1   **Planning is helpful.** Encourage trainees to spend a few minutes sketching out their work before they start using the computer. It is possible (and easy) to modify a spreadsheet if it isn't set out correctly, but it is worth avoiding this with a little thought.

2   **Sort out the arithmetic first.** As with all computer applications, the computer does exactly what it is told! It is vital that your trainees understand the process that is to be carried out on the data so that they can tell the computer what to do. It is useful to do some of the calculations on paper before using the computer and using the results as a check that the computer is giving the correct answers.

3   **Use the keyboard for data entry.** If the mouse is used all the time, data entry is very slow, as a hand has to be taken on and off the keyboard continually. The arrow keys on the keyboard are quicker for moving the cursor small distances. The mouse is often quicker for moving a long way, or for selecting blocks of cells.

4   **The numeric keypad is quickest for entering numbers.** Most computer keypads include a numeric keypad with the numbers set out in a standard pattern. This is quicker to use than the numbers on the top row of keys which are above the letters on the keyboard. The basic arithmetic signs are there too. If the cursor moves when they try to use this keypad, pressing the key labelled 'Num Lock' may sort it out.

5   **Show your trainees that it doesn't matter if columns are too narrow.** A common worry with beginners is that some of their data is too wide for the columns of the spreadsheet. Show them that this doesn't matter: the calculations will still be correct. On modern spreadsheets it is very easy to change column widths, so show them this at a fairly early stage.

6   **Use simple calculations at first.** If basic arithmetic is used for the first few exercises, it will build confidence. It is also simple to check that the results of calculations are correct.

7   **Show trainees where their 'lost' data has gone.** In the early stage of spreadsheet use, a common difficulty is disappearing data. People don't realize how big the spreadsheet is and scroll to an empty part of the spreadsheet by accident. Make sure that they know that the working area is much bigger than the screen and that they can use the row and column numbers and letters to keep track of where they are. Another problem is opening another spreadsheet by accident and obscuring the one with the data on it.

8   **Encourage the correct formatting of data.** It is easy to control the appearance of data by setting the number of decimal places wanted, or by using a currency format. These details help make a spreadsheet look good and make it easy to read correctly. It is also easy to use different fonts and colours, as well as putting borders around tables. It is important that this is kept tasteful!

9   **Control over printing should be covered at an early stage.** Many spreadsheets are too wide to fit on a 'portrait' page, but will fit well on a 'landscape' one. Show your trainees how to do this and how they can use smaller fonts and narrow columns to fit more on to a page. If the spreadsheet is too big to fit on one page, they will need to know how to print it in instalments, with appropriate headings and page numbers.

10   **Explain the importance of absolute cell references.** If an application demands that a number is used several times in a spreadsheet, it is best that it is only entered into one cell and always used from that cell. An example of this is the VAT rate. If this was entered into several places in a spreadsheet, there could be problems if it was changed. By entering it once, it is very easy to alter. This can be a difficult concept to grasp and should not be tackled until the basics are well understood. It is, however, vital for effective spreadsheet use.

11   **Demonstrate how charts and graphs can be produced from spreadsheets.** It is very easy to produce clear charts to summarize spreadsheet data. They can be used for presentations and they can also be pasted into word processed documents.

23

Training about databases

Databases complete the trio of basic computer applications. They are used to store, manipulate and retrieve data, like an electronic equivalent of a manual file card system. Because the power of the computer is available, it is possible to perform tasks that would be difficult with a manual system. These tasks include sorting data into a different order, extracting part of the data or performing complex searches. Many database packages also have facilities for linking two or more data files together for more sophisticated applications. At the highest level of database use, a programming language can be used to automate complex tasks.

1   **Encourage planning.** Before trainees start to construct a new database, ask them to design its structure on paper. Although it is possible to go back and alter the design when it is on the computer, it will be quicker to do it correctly the first time.

2   **Make sure they choose field names carefully.** If field names are too long and descriptive, they will make the design untidy and fill the screen with clutter. On the other hand, if they are too cryptic, they may have trouble remembering what they are if they go back to them six months later.

3   **Using the correct field type is important.** Database programs use a wide range of field types. Check that your trainees use the correct type so that they can enter data easily and achieve the results they need. For example, numbers can be entered into text fields but cannot be used for calculations, so you should use a numeric field for them.

4   **Show them how to use 'choice' fields whenever possible.** 'Choice' fields let you enter data by selecting it from a list. If a field only has a limited range of possibilities (such as SEX – Male or Female are the only acceptable entries), restricting data entry to a list of choices will reduce errors. If the choices available are long (or difficult to spell), typing will also be easier.

5   **Help trainees to think about how data will be updated.** A good example of the problems that can arise is the use of an 'Age' field. Data may be correct when it is entered, but a year later, all the entries will be wrong. It is far better to use a 'Date of Birth' field and get the computer to calculate the age automatically.

6   **Encourage good design of data entry screens.** When the user is entering data, it is confusing if the cursor jumps around the screen as fields are filled. Ideally, the cursor should move straight down a single column. If there are too many fields for this, fill one column before starting the other, or use two screens for data entry.

7   **Warn about being careful when entering data.** If a trainee is not a touch typist and is not watching the screen, it is easy to enter data into the wrong field. This is a particular problem if the cursor moves on automatically when a field is full. If this isn't realized and the return key is pressed, a field is skipped.

8   **Make sure the correct fields are included in each database.** The main purpose of a database is to output the data that is needed, in the form in which it is wanted. In order to achieve this the correct data must be included, so it is important that no fields are left out. There is, however, no point in storing data which will never be needed.

9   **Show the different options for outputting data.** It can be difficult to fit all the data required onto a screen or a printout. It is very useful to be aware of all the different options for formatting the output so that it fits sensibly on to the screen or page.

10   **Save relational databases until your trainees are confident with the basics.** Relational databases link files together to provide more sophisticated designs. Make sure that your trainees are thoroughly conversant with simple, 'flat file' databases before attempting to show them relational databases. Start the relational topic with some simple examples and show how they can be used to avoid 'redundant' data.

24

Training about programming

Programming is probably the most complex of all the uses of computers. Before trainees start to learn about it, they should be familiar with using computers as an everyday tool and competent users of the three main computer applications already discussed in this chapter.

1   **Make sure that your trainees really need to learn to program.** Programming a complex task is very difficult and it will take a long time to learn to do this effectively. Before deciding to teach a language, make sure that the tasks the trainees want to do can't be done by a computer application. Many of these applications can perform very sophisticated tasks and these can often be made more powerful by using the application's own programming language.

2   **Take care over the selection of the language that you are going to teach.** There is a very large number of different programming languages available. These vary greatly in their complexity and in the tasks for which they are suited. You will also need to make sure that you know enough about the language to be able to teach it effectively!

3   **Insist on good design before a program is started.** It is only worth writing a program when there is a complex task to be performed. Attempts to produce complex programs without designing them first will fail, so insist on good design from the start.

4   **Make sure that your trainees understand computer logic.** Computers are very good at performing logical operations and this is the basis of their power. Programmers need to be able to understand this logic and to use it correctly so as to utilize this power.

5   **Make sure that your trainees produce well structured programs.** If a computer program is very complex, it can also be very hard to understand. This may not be a problem when the program is being written, but it may be almost impossible to modify the program at a later date. A well structured program will be broken down into smaller blocks, each of which performs a specific task and is relatively easy to understand. Programming languages differ in how easy it is to structure programs and how the structuring is carried out.

6   **Make sure that programs are documented.** It is important that a programmer keeps notes about how programs are written and what different parts of the programs do. These notes should be written up into proper documentation so that the programs can be understood at a later date. Ideally, there should be a standard form of documentation so that a different programmer could use it to modify the programs in the future. Very few people like documenting their work, so you may need to insist that it is done.

7   **Insist that programs can be modified easily.** If programs are well written, it should be easy to change some basic features of how they operate. As an example, it should be possible to change the screen colour by making an alteration in one place in the program. A bad program might need several alterations to achieve the same thing.

8   **Encourage reuse of useful parts of programs.** Rather than starting a new program from scratch, it is often possible to use parts of another program and add in the bits needed for the new one. If a program is well documented and structured and is easily modified, this should be fairly easy to do.

9   **Insist on thorough testing.** Before programs are used for their intended tasks, it is vital to check that they work properly. When data are input, the correct results must happen. Equally importantly, programs must be able to cope with invalid data being entered. Testing of programs must be carefully designed to make sure that they give a suitable response if an error is encountered.

10 **Input and output must be carried out in a suitable manner.** In order to reduce errors, it must be easy for operators to enter data into the correct fields and to be given warnings if the data entries they key in are invalid. It is also important that the output is in the format that the users want.

Chapter 4   Looking after your Stress Levels!

So far in this book, we have concentrated on giving your trainees a productive and effective learning experience with computers or about computers. In this chapter, we want to try to help *you*! So, most of our suggestions are about looking after yourself, both before and during routine training sessions on familiar territory, and also about travelling to train at distant or unknown venues.

We start with suggestions about 'Getting there early and setting up', which are particularly designed for when you are working away from your normal base, and need to get tuned into the environment and facilities with which you will be working.

Our next two sets of suggestions are about damage limitation in disasters. When the power goes off, trainers using computers in their work are disadvantaged much more than if they had only been using flipcharts and markerboards. Such things, however, are likely to come into their own as fallback devices with which to replan your session when other facilities become unavailable.

We move on to look at ways of working with difficult trainees. The two extremes tend to be the technophobes, who can take a lot of coaxing before they relax their inhibitions regarding computers and communications technologies. At the other extreme (and just as trying!) are the technophiles. These are the trainees who always seem to know just a little more about the technology than you do.

The remainder of this chapter is about being an international trainer – or at least about organizing the first two or three jaunts to foreign parts to work. 'Looking after yourself when travelling' offers suggestions for saving your energies for the actual training session, if you find yourself working at a distance, maybe abroad, and in a different climate. The complementary side of such work is to do with all the bits and pieces that you may need, either to take with you or to arrange to be at your distant venue. We don't claim to have covered everything in 'Gadgets, leads and grommets', or 'Finding out what they've got at their end', but we hope that we will alert you to some of the main things you need to consider, and thereby help you to reduce your stress levels when working away from home. Finally, 'Finding out what you can take elsewhere' aims to help you avoid stressful situations when travelling abroad to work, not least by helping to spare you from expending energy by carrying items which could prove unusable.

25

Getting there early and setting up

There are few worse nightmares for trainers than that of arriving late at your training venue, and then finding that the equipment you've been depending upon is not there, or not working. These are particularly worrying when you are working away from your normal base, and even more so if you're working abroad! The following suggestions may help you to avoid some of your nightmares becoming realities.

1   **Make checklists of all the bits and pieces that you will need.** Divide this into two parts: things *you* will have with you, and things you need to be available on site in the training room. As you prepare for your session, tick off on your list all the things you will be taking with you, and when you get to the venue, tick off the remaining items on your list. This saves the embarrassment of getting midway through a training session, and then discovering that there's something missing, and being *seen* to have messed things up!

2   **Liaise in advance if you are working in a distant venue.** Book all of the equipment you are likely to need. This is particularly important when you're planning to use a computer to support your presentation. Find out about compatibility with your own equipment, and with your own software. You may be able simply to take along your PowerPoint presentation on disk, for example, if you already know that the software (in the same version as you use) is installed on equipment in the training room.

3   **Check up *again* a week or two before your training session.** It is always worth reminding people at the venue about your requirements. Just occasionally, the records of what you wanted will have entirely disappeared!

4   **Plan your fallback position.** For example, make sure that there will be an overhead projector and flipchart in the room. This provides peace of mind, and saves you worrying too much about what you will do if the computer side of your requirements does not turn out to be there. Even if you only use the traditional equipment for the first hour or so (while someone sorts out the computing side for you), it means that you can get your session under way on time.

5   **Arrive at your training venue in good time.** About an hour early is usually right, especially if travel is involved. Even if the room is occupied by some other session when you arrive, it is better to be having a cup of coffee nearby, than to be wondering if you will get there in time to set up.

6   **Make full use of local help in setting up.** The people who normally look after the training room may already know only too well any idiosyncrasies or quirks of the equipment that is there. Don't exclude them from your setting up, even if you're very confident that you know how to get everything working. You may need their help again if anything breaks down.

7   **Test out visibility.** Choose the part of your presentation that might be the most difficult to see, and check that it is legible from any part of the training room, adjusting the furniture accordingly if necessary.

8   **Get your backup ready too.** Check the overhead projector, and position it so that you can easily bring it into play if you need it. Get out at least some of your transparencies, in case you need them at short notice if something goes wrong with the other equipment.

9   **Make sure that you can't lose anything irretrievably.** For example, if your PowerPoint presentation is on a disk that you are putting into someone else's equipment, have a copy with you just in case that disk corrupts or gets erased accidentally.

10 **Learn from your own disasters!** When something goes wrong, and a session is interrupted or has to be replanned at short notice, it is tempting to try to forget the experience. It is, however, worthwhile to keep a short summary of 'lessons learnt for the future', and to look again at this from time to time to make sure that you don't make the same mistake twice.

26

What to do if there's a power cut!

Loss of electricity is not a frequent occurrence, but it is one of most trainers' nightmares, especially when using computer-aided presentations or demonstrations away from home. The following suggestions may help you to keep your show on the road until normal service is resumed.

1   **Check quickly that it's not an emergency.** Power may go off because there's a fire in the building, or because an accident has happened somewhere. Without panicking your trainees, or rushing them out of the room, find out whether you need to leave the venue and, if so, forget everything else and concentrate on getting everyone out safely and quickly.

2   **Don't panic when the power goes off.** It may well mean that you will need to restructure your training session, but it doesn't mean that you will have to abandon it (unless, of course, there is no lighting at all left in the room). Getting flustered and cross does not help to make your training session a success. Stay cool.

3   **Take a break.** If you know that it's going to take you a few minutes to devise a backup plan for the session, give yourself some time and space to get on with this. Your trainees won't be devastated by the prospect of a few minutes off while you organize some alternatives.

4   **Plan some paper-based exercises which could cover some of the same ground as your training session.** You may be using some of these in any case, to add variety to your trainees' learning experience. In particular, have some things ready for your trainees to do, so that you can report the power failure and try to get it restored. At such times, it can be really useful to introduce a syndicate task, as this keeps your trainees busy and talking, rather than sitting waiting for the equipment to work again.

5   **Switch off projectors, computers and so on at the mains.** There is always the possibility of the power coming back with a surge, and that could cause far more damage than a cut. Some software does not like being shut down unexpectedly, and you may need to be prepared to spend some time setting it up again when the power is restored.

6   **If necessary, take your group somewhere else.** If the room is too dark to work in, for example, find somewhere else in the building which has some light, or a lounge area, where you can continue at least in part with your intended session.

7   **Continue on flipchart and whiteboard.** Keep the session active by asking your trainees to prioritize options, do brainstorms, make action plans, and so on. Make sure that the products of their activities continue to be available to them, such as by sticking flipcharts around the walls.

8   **Consider doing some revision and consolidation.** This is always useful, and it is a productive way of making use of enforced interruptions in your training session. Get trainees to sum up what was the most important thing that they have learnt so far, and get them to work out questions about what they need to find out next.

9   **Declare another coffee break when the power comes back on.** Alternatively, give your trainees a few minutes to stretch their legs or look at some other training materials in the room. This gives you the chance to get your equipment switched on and ready for use, and is much more comfortable than trying to do so with everyone's eyes on you.

10   **Don't just restart exactly where you left off.** It can be worthwhile to restart at the position a few minutes *before* the power went off, so that your trainees can pick up the threads of what they were thinking when it happened.

27

Replanning your session

Technology is wonderful, when it is all there, all working and all familiar. However, life isn't always so easy! There are times when we all have to go back to blackboards or whiteboards and overhead projectors. The following suggestions may help you to keep your show on the road when the road seems blocked!

1   **Never depend on being able to do a computer-managed presentation.** Most of the time there will be no problem, but on that occasion where it just isn't going to work, be ready to go ahead using an overhead projector, or even on whiteboard or flipchart if no visual aids are available. Always carry the main part of your presentation on a few carefully chosen overheads, just in case.

2   **Keep your backup resources ready for immediate use.** It could be that you've not used your emergency overheads for months, but it's still worth having them in a sensible order, so that you can locate any one of them at short notice. You will not always need emergency backup from the beginning of a session, and it looks much more professional if when things break down in the middle of a session you are able to find exactly the right place to pick up in another medium where you were interrupted with the previous medium.

3   **Have with you some backup activities as well as backup resources.** When there are parts of your planned programme that *you* just can't do, it is important to be able to fill your trainees' time usefully. Think of some group tasks or exercises that will help them get a firm grip on the basics, that can replace some of the time when you might otherwise have shown them some of the finer points about the topic of the session.

4   **Don't shoot the messenger.** When things don't work out, it can be tempting to grumble about the facilities at your training venue, or about things that were promised for you not turning out to be available. Getting cross with people does not do you any good, and your trainees will be much more impressed if you calmly and cheerfully get on with your training session using other means.

5   **Don't spend too long trying to get things working.** Even if you are fairly certain that it will only take another five minutes to get all of the equipment working, five minutes can be a long time for your trainees to watch you trying to sort things out, and there is every chance that it will then take much longer anyway. It is better to get started with your session on time, and to fiddle about with the equipment again (if at all) when your trainees are busy in a task, particularly a group task where they will be much less likely to take any notice of your activities with the equipment.

6   **Replan the content of your session.** Don't put yourself in the position of saying, 'now if we'd had the computer backup, what we'd have done would be...' Your trainees aren't interested in what you would have done. Simply get on with providing as good a session as you can to meet the original aims and objectives. This will often mean missing out altogether some things that you would otherwise have done. It may also mean designing quickly some new task briefings for your trainees, so that they can go ahead even without some of the material you would otherwise have given them or shown them.

7   **Make your (revised) objectives clear.** If you can no longer show these on overhead or computer-projection, it is well worth writing them up on a marker board or flipchart, so that they remain visible to your trainees throughout your replanned session. It is usually possible to get this done before the session starts. Be prepared to ditch any particular objectives which it would no longer be possible to achieve, and replace these with others that are relevant and useful to your trainees. You may be able to cover the missed ground on a future occasion, but in any case there's not much point talking about things that you are unable to do in the present session.

8   **Write up task briefings.** Word of mouth is not usually enough. If you would originally have displayed task briefings on overhead or screen, it is worth writing them up on flipcharts, so that your trainees have no doubt about what you intend them to do for each task in your session. You can write the briefing for the next task while they are working on the present one.

9   **Make good use of your handout materials.** For example, you may have planned to give out a handout version of your PowerPoint presentation as a revision aid after your talk. If the technology is not available, it may still be possible to issue your handouts straightaway, then talk your trainees through their copies of your slides, getting them to annotate the copies with their own notes with the most important things as you go along.

10   **Use any spare time to find out more about your trainees' learning and experience.** It can be really useful to have the luxury of some time to find out in some detail who knows what, for example, about the work you may be covering in a future planned session with the same trainees. You may also find time to give them some revision or practice exercises in areas that you have already covered with them.

28

Coping with technophobes

In many groups of trainees, there will be a few who are convinced that they cannot work with technology. This fear may be very deep seated and you will have to work very hard to help them to overcome it. The following suggestions may give you some ways of starting to overcome their fears.

1 **Remind them of the difficulties people face in learning new skills.** People are always taking on new challenges that seem impossible at first. If they are persistent enough, they can surprise themselves. Remind your trainees that they have already learnt far more complex topics, such as learning to walk, talk, ride a bike or drive a car. These tasks seemed impossibly difficult at first, but with practice they can become automatic functions.

2 **Encourage trainees to think of computers as tools for doing a job.** If the computer is a tool, there is no need to understand how it works. The only knowledge necessary is how to use the tool and how to maintain it properly. If it helps to explain this, use analogies such as a car: there is no need to know exactly how it works in order to drive it. Similarly, there is no need to know how a hammer is made in order to drive in nails.

3 **Try to structure learning well so that each stage builds on and reinforces prior learning.** It is important that the trainees' understanding of basic principles is good and that they have plenty of practice before moving on to new topics. If they move on to new areas too soon, the seeds of future confusion can be sown. It is also very useful to incorporate lessons from early work into later stages as well, so that revision is carried out.

4 **Make sure that trainees realize that computers do exactly as they are told.** It is common for people to say that 'the computer' did something. This sort of thought can encourage them to believe that the machine is outside their control and acts by itself. It is very important that they should realize that the computer does exactly as it is told. If something unexpected happens, it is as a result of something the computer has been instructed to do, and there is an explanation for it.

5   **Be prepared to help trainees carry out a 'post mortem' when things go wrong.** By talking through what has happened with the trainee and by using any 'undo' facilities, it may be possible to illustrate exactly what has gone wrong. Software may also have facilities which show more clearly what is going on: examples are showing spaces and returns in word processors, and showing formulae in spreadsheets.

6   **Try to relate computer uses to the tasks trainees may need for their work.** If they can see a real point to using computers, trainees will have more incentive to learn. Try to find exercises that will help trainees to see how relevant computing can be to them.

7   **Make sure that trainees don't worry too much about complex problems during the early stages.** People will often realize that they have been set a simplified task and that the real world is more complex. This may lead them to attempt a more advanced solution than you had planned, leading to difficulties and confusion. Try to word tasks so that they make it clear what level of complexity is involved.

8   **Set appropriate challenges.** In order for trainees to learn, they must solve problems. These problems should be hard enough to encourage thought, but they must be achievable by the individual. It will take considerable thought to choose tasks that match the needs of each trainee.

9   **Review progress regularly and give praise.** When a trainee achieves something, help them realize what they have done. Remind them of all the skills that they used in the task, and contrast this with their skill level when they started. It might be useful to make this a formal process, with regular reviews of learning and the filling in of some kind of skills record.

10 **Celebrate achievement.** Make sure trainees give themselves credit for their achievements and that they don't compare themselves with others in the group. It is common for people to feel inferior to others who learn faster, or who are more technically literate when they start the course. What is important is their own progress, not the achievements of others.

29

Coping with technophiles

People who love computers can become a problem, especially when they know more about IT than you do! It is common for a group to contain some individuals who have considerable IT skills. There are two ways in which they can be a problem: they can become bored, and they can be disruptive. It is not an easy job to decide the best way to deal with this and you may need all your tact.

1 **Carry out some assessment of prior knowledge at an early stage.** In order to identify those who have good computing skills, you will need to ask questions. You could do this informally with a few spoken questions. You could also have a form which trainees fill in before the course in order to clarify this. Care should be taken that a form doesn't imply that trainees will need good computing skills, or beginners may be put off.

2 **Test that trainees really have the skills that they claim.** People sometimes have an unrealistic view of their skills so you need to check that they can really do all that they claim. Set these people some tasks that will allow them to demonstrate these skills. Avoid any suggestion that you are testing them: say that you are assessing their prior learning in order to help you plan their future work.

3 **Don't try to fool them if you aren't sure of the subject.** It can be embarrassing to admit that you don't know something if you are providing training. If you try to bluff somebody who has better knowledge than you, failure is likely. This is even more embarrassing. A better solution is to offer to find the answer to questions or problems for the next session.

4 **Remember that training skills are just as important as advanced subject knowledge.** Your confidence may be dented if you find that some of your trainees know more about that subject than you do. Remind yourself that you are multi-skilled: you have computing knowledge and you are skilled as a trainer. Use your training skills in order to help you to provide effective computer training. As an analogy, think about world class athletes. They rely on trainers who help them develop their competitive skills, but these trainers aren't top athletes themselves.

5   **See if they can help others who have less knowledge.** If some trainees have skills, they could use them to help those who may be struggling. This can be very helpful to all concerned: your life can be easier, the beginners receive more help, and the advanced ones can crystallize their knowledge by explaining it to someone else. You will still need to supervise this help, however, to make sure it is effective.

6   **Ask them to prepare a session on an advanced topic that they could teach to the others.** If you can choose a topic beyond their current knowledge, it will be useful for them to learn it and they can then practise some training skills for the benefit of the rest of the group when they are ready. You can learn from them, too!

7   **Set them a complex task to keep them quiet.** If you are having trouble because some people are causing disruption, consider setting them a task that will stretch their abilities. This can help keep them occupied, but they will still be learning.

8   **Ask the trainees concerned what they hope to achieve from attending the course.** This might help focus the disruptive trainees' minds on what they are doing and encourage them to take an active part in it. If nothing else, it might help you to clarify a particular trainee's needs.

9   **If it is appropriate, suggest that they consider a more advanced course.** This will need diplomacy, but you could stress that they will not gain anything from the course as they have all the skills already. It would be a more productive use of their time if they were to do a course at a more suitable level.

10 **If all else fails, speak to their supervisor.** If you are having problems with one or more trainees being disruptive because they feel superior about their advanced knowledge, you must deal with the problem in order to be fair to the others. If all the techniques above have failed, consider an approach to the trainee's supervisor, perhaps suggesting that the course you are presenting is not suitable for this trainee.

30

Looking after yourself when travelling

Travelling trainers are probably as common now as travelling salespeople once were. If your work has you on the road for a significant part of your time, it pays dividends to make sure that the travelling side of things causes you as little stress as is possible. The following suggestions may offer you some low stress alternatives.

1   **Think seriously about using public transport.** If you have long distances to travel and can get to where you need to go by train, for example, this can reduce the strain on you. It means that you can rest on the way home, rather than have the strain of driving when you're already tired after a day's training. However, it's worth setting out in good time on your way to your training event, as the strain of the train being late could be even worse!

2   **However you travel, aim to arrive at your training venue with plenty of time to spare.** Being late is stressful, but *knowing* that you're going to be late is even more stressful. If there is a distinct possibility of you being late, and you can't compensate for this by setting out early, it can be worth trying to arrange for contingencies, for example, with a substitute who can start off your session if you are delayed *en route*, or who can give your trainees a relevant task to do in anticipation of your session.

3   **Watch your diary if you're very itinerant!** It's only too easy to see a blank day and say 'yes' to an engagement in Aberdeen, but not to notice that you're in Birmingham the day before or Brighton the day after! Travel takes time, and if you've got long distances to go, you might have to devote some days just to travelling.

4   **Try to travel relatively light.** This is particularly important when using public transport, or when flying. While it's reassuring to have with you everything you might possibly need for your training event, it is tiring

carrying it all around with you. Large collections of overhead trans-parencies can be surprisingly heavy, as can multiple copies of handout material, or examples of books and manuals.

5   **Look after your temperature.** When choosing clothing for training and travel, it's useful to have the option to cope with unexpected heat or cold, and to pack the sorts of clothes that allow you to add or shed a layer when necessary. This can be particularly important if your trip takes in different climates, but even in one part of the world temperatures in training venues can vary quite considerably.

6   **Look after routine minor ailment possibilities.** It can be a real blessing to have with you small quantities of aspirin or paracetamol for the odd headache or cold, a few throat lozenges for the possibility of a sore voice, something for an upset stomach, and so on. Even if *you* don't need these emergency supplies, you may be surprised at how often you can help someone else out because of them.

7   **Carry some emergency repair materials.** A needle and thread can make all the difference to your composure in the event of a button coming off, or a seam coming undone. It can also help to have that spare button, a couple of safety pins, a few tissues for cleaning off spilt food or drinks, and so on. Most hotels have supplies of basic essentials at reception, but not all training centres carry such materials.

8   **Keep your toiletries packed if you travel regularly.** It's useful to have a small separate toiletries bag, and to keep it maintained with sufficient supplies for a few days away from home. This can save you having to spend time and energy worrying about packing toothpaste, a toothbrush, shampoo, soap, and all the other bits and pieces that you never notice when you have them, but are a pain when you find you haven't got them. Aim for just having to remember to pack *one* thing – the bag – but check that you take the right one!

9   **Remember about jet lag if you travel long distances.** Moving to a completely different time zone affects some people much more than others, but it's worth giving yourself a day without meetings or training sessions so that you can catch up on sleep and adjust at least partially. It's not always possible to sleep on long plane journeys, often because of other passengers.

10 **Carry some ear plugs.** Alternatively, the in-ear phones that connect to portable cassette or compact disk players will do. These can cut down the disturbance to you caused by fellow passengers, or can help you to sleep in hotel rooms where there may be various sounds that, because they are unfamiliar, can keep you awake.

31

Gadgets, leads and grommets

If you travel to deliver training, it is very important that you think carefully about what you need to take with you. If you're taking several of the things listed below, the public transport suggestion in our previous set of tips will be ruled out! If you take too much with you, it will be heavy and at risk of damage or loss. If you forget something, you won't be able to go back for it and you may not be able to borrow or buy it locally. Even if you have asked the people at your destination about their facilities, it is possible to forget something vital; take steps to cover yourself against problems.

1   **Think about those who are left behind.** If you need to take equipment away with you to carry out some training, make sure that it won't be needed by other people at your base. If you take it away, leaving others stranded, you will lose popularity!

2   **A spare mains lead can be useful when travelling abroad.** If your mains adaptor doesn't work, you could ask a technician to put a suitable plug on your extra mains lead. This would ensure reliable operation. If the mains lead incorporates a power supply, this option may not be possible and you might not want to take the risk of having the UK plug cut off your only power supply!

3   **Take some fuses with you.** Electrical systems abroad will use different sizes of fuses. Take some with you, so that you can replace them if they blow.

4   **Make sure you have plenty of batteries.** If you want to use equipment while you are travelling, or if you want to use batteries to avoid mains problems, you will need enough batteries to operate without interruptions. Be wary of manufacturers' claims for how long their equipment will run on one battery charge.

5   **Don't forget your battery charger.** If you foresee a need to charge up large numbers of batteries, you may even need to take an extra charger, or one that can charge more than one battery at a time.

6   **Make sure you have plenty of ink cartridges if you are taking a printer.** Some printers are very small and light, so taking one with you is not impossible. If you run out of ink, however, it will become a useless dead weight!

7   **Take loads of leads with you.** If you think you might want to connect your computer to other equipment, try to think of all the possible variations of leads that might be needed. As an example, you might want to use a modem: take 25 pin and 9 pin serial leads with you.

8   **Consider taking a 'palmtop' computer to test this out for future work.** If the thought of taking all this equipment with you is daunting, you might be able to take a very small, light palmtop computer. You would need to be absolutely certain that it would connect up to the system at your destination, however. If you want to try this, take one with you on an early visit to test that it all works.

9   **Perhaps you only need a disk or two.** If you don't need a computer on your journey, you might be able to take all the data and software you need on disk. If you need a large amount of disk space, you could take a portable exchangeable disk system. They are very light and can often be connected to the printer port of computers. Again, you should test this before relying on it.

10 **Do you need to carry anything at all?** As you are a highly sophisticated computer user, why not benefit from modern high speed data communications? Instead of carrying data with you, e-mail it to your destination. Check that it has arrived safely, however. Perhaps you should take a backup, too!

32

Finding out what they've got at their end

The next pages contain some questions you should ask before setting out to distant parts to deliver training. Most of the questions apply to visiting countries abroad, but some of them are just as important to ask if you're planning some training in a distant venue in your own country.

1   **What is the specification of the computers?** It is important to make sure that any software or data that you take with you will work properly. It will be helpful to know the make and model of the computers, what processor they are using and how much memory they have.

2   **What operating system do they use?** Again, it is important that you know this for compatibility purposes. Make sure you know what version it is. If it is a version which has been produced specially for that country, it may have important differences from your version.

3   **What software is installed on the computers?** You will need to know what versions are available and possibly in what language. Spell checking with a 'foreign' word processor is not a viable option!

4   **Are the computers networked?** If you want to connect your computer to a network, you will need to know details of their system so that you can make sure that you have the necessary hardware and software . This can also be important if you want to add typefaces or software to the system.

5   **Is there some kind of interchangeable hard disk system available?** These can be very useful if you want to take large amounts of data with you. Make sure yours is compatible or, alternatively, check that you can take a portable unit with you to plug into their machines.

6   **Will there be technical help available?** If there are problems, you will need help from the local staff to solve them. An important point to note is that systems can be password protected and you will not be able to alter them without authorization.

7   **What sort of printing facilities are available?** You may want trainees to print out their work, or you may want to produce some extra notes and print them. You may want to reprint your presentation on overhead projector transparencies from your backup on disk. Some knowledge of the printing system will help you to plan.

8   **What projection systems are there?** You may want to use an overhead projector to show your presentation, or to connect your laptop to a large screen or projector. Make sure that you know what will be provided.

9   **What voltage and frequency is the electricity supply?** Make sure that your equipment will operate under these conditions. Check your manual, or speak to a local service agent to make sure that there will not be problems.

10 **What sort of mains outlets are there?** An adaptor may be needed, but check what kind it is. It's useful to get your own adaptor, plus a normal multi-socket outlet, so that you can connect more than one of your pieces of equipment to a single foreign socket. This may also be useful for your travel kettle, computer and mobile phone charger in your hotel room!

33

Finding out what you can take elsewhere

You may already be accustomed to training in different countries, or you may have no plans to venture abroad. If neither of these apply, you may find the first time that you take your show abroad rather daunting. We hope that the following suggestions may minimize some of the potential problems that you might encounter.

1   **Be careful about customs regulations.** If you take equipment to some countries, you risk having it confiscated or paying duties on it. Find out about regulations, and make sure you fill in any forms that you need to use.

2   **Make sure that the equipment will work with the power supply in the country you intend to visit.** Some countries have electricity supplies that work at different voltages and frequencies. Make sure that you know what sort of supplies are available and that your equipment will cope with it.

3   **Check that your equipment will deal with power fluctuations.** Some electricity supplies are liable to fluctuations. These will not upset most electrical items, but computers can have problems with them. There are some simple devices available that will help smooth out minor variations and help your computer to operate properly. These devices can also protect your computer from surges in the electricity supply that could damage your equipment.

4   **Battery power can help you if there are electricity problems.** A battery charger is less likely to be upset by electrical mains fluctuations than a computer is. You could recharge the batteries overnight and then use them during the day. You will need to take plenty of batteries with you, and make sure that you have adaptors to work the charger.

5   **Take suitable mains adaptors with you.** There is a wide range of different mains sockets in the countries of the world. You will need to make sure that you have a suitable adaptor with you. If you have several items of mains operated equipment, you could take a multi-socket outlet with you so that you can run the equipment from one adaptor.

6   **Find out if there is a recognized repairer for your equipment in the places you intend to visit.** Many computer firms have an international network of service agents for their equipment. If you have the details of these, you could contact them if your equipment fails.

7   **Check up very carefully on possible compatibility problems.** If you intend to connect your equipment to any other items at your destination, make sure that you have all the adaptors and connectors that will be necessary. If you intend to use any software or data files, you will also need to check that your work is compatible and uses the same operating system.

8   **Take backups of data and software with you.** It is a good policy to have backups of your work all the time, but this is particularly true when you are abroad. Backups are light to carry, so won't add much to your load. Carry backups in your hand luggage, in case the rest of your luggage goes missing.

9   **Take backups of important leads and connectors too.** Again, these are light so it is easy to carry them. They should also be carried in your hand luggage.

10   **Be careful with data held on magnetic disks.** There is a small risk that the X-ray equipment used for security checks could damage data held on magnetic disks. You can protect them in special bags and also ask to have your hand luggage checked by hand.

11   **Take data in as many different file formats as possible.** By saving data in different formats, you have as much flexibility as possible to help in overcoming compatibility problems. As an example, you can save word processed documents in plain text and Rich Text Format (RTF) from many word processors. These formats are widely used and may enable a document to load into a different word processor.

12   **Allow plenty of time to sort out compatibility problems.** If there are problems, it can be very difficult to solve them. You may need to seek help from a local expert and it may be hard to find somebody. Even if you can open files, you may find that they need to be edited because of different fonts changing the layout of documents. Word processed documents may lose some of their formatting because of problems with compatibility.

13   **Take a virus checker.** Viruses are always a danger and you should take all the precautions that you can. Make sure your own computer is virus protected and check any files before using them.

Chapter 5   Using Communications Technologies

Information and communications technologies have, of course, already been touched on in various parts of this book. This chapter is our attempt to bring together some of the main considerations of using e-mail, computer conferencing and the Internet to support trainees' learning. In practice, these information and communications technologies are so interrelated that it is difficult to split them up and address them separately. Nevertheless, we have tried to do so, for the sake of readers of this book who may be coming to them one at a time or in a particular order, but inevitably there is overlap between some of our suggestions, and we suggest that if you are new to these technologies, you scan the whole chapter first before homing into the part that may be a priority for you now.

Our first three sets of suggestions are about e-mail. We've called it 'e-mail' throughout this book, although it is now becoming usual for people who are well into it to drop the hyphen and use the word email instead. We offer suggestions about making good use of e-mail yourself, then getting trainees started on e-mail themselves. We offer an extended set of suggestions about one of the most productive uses of e-mail in training, that of giving trainees individual feedback on their own work using the technology. These suggestions lead us in to computer conferencing, so next we offer suggestions about setting up and using computer conferencing. This builds on to many of the tips about using e-mail offered earlier in the chapter, and also extends our advice offered in Chapter 1 about getting trainees to work together at a distance.

We end this chapter with three sets of suggestions exploring different aspects of using the Internet for training and learning.

34

Making effective use of e-mail

E-mail is the simplest form of communicating by computer. Electronic communication is addictive! To most people who have already climbed the learning curve of finding out how to use e-mail, the apprehension they may have experienced on their first encounters fades into insignificance. E-mail can be an important medium in training. Computers can be linked up to a network and the users are issued with e-mail addresses. A user can use e-mail software to type a message and send it to any other user. The message is stored on a central computer until the recipient collects it. This can be on a computer network within a company, or it can be via the Internet. The Internet will enable users anywhere in the world to exchange messages. Once you are connected to the Internet, sending e-mail is cheaper than sending a letter or making a telephone call and is much quicker. The following suggestions may help you to get started with e-mail yourself, and to maximize some of the benefits that e-mail can offer to you and to your trainees.

1   **Find out what e-mail facilities your institution has available.** If you work in an organization, it may already have access to e-mail facilities. It may be possible for you to use these facilities, saving you the effort of organizing your own.

2   **Arrange to have your own e-mail address.** It is much better to be able to collect your e-mail separately from the rest of your organization. This will help avoid e-mail being lost within the organization and will help others feel that they are communicating with you directly.

3   **Choose your e-mail address carefully.** You may be able to choose the first part of your own address. Make sure that it uses the name you usually use for your communications. It is common for IT managers to issue e-mail addresses to people based on their names from a personnel file. As an example, if your name is *Keith Robert Simpson*, the first part of the e-mail address you are issued might be *KR Simpson*. If you are generally known as *Bob*, people will not recognize you from the e-mail address. If it is possible, insist that the name part of your e-mail address is what you want it to be.

4   **Include your e-mail address on written communications and tell people it when you are on the telephone.** Make the address part of your letterhead so as to make it widely known. Encourage people to e-mail you, rather than writing to you or telephoning you.

5   **Take care to let people know if your e-mail address changes.** If you move from one service provider to another, for example, or if your institution changes its address details, your e-mail address will change. It can be worth the time spent to e-mail everyone in your address book with details of any forthcoming change, and then to e-mail them again from your new address as soon as the change is implemented.

6   **Ask other people if they have e-mail and what their addresses are.** Most e-mail software includes an electronic address book. You can enter the e-mail addresses into it when you are told them. When you want to send an e-mail message, you can just select who you want to send it to and the computer will fill the address in for you.

7   **Make sure that trainees get started with e-mail.** Write careful, step-by-step briefing instructions for your trainees. The computer literate people may hardly do more than glance at these before getting into the swing of using e-mail. However, for those people who lack confidence or experience with computers, these instructions can be vital and comforting until they become familiar with the medium.

8   **Decide what you really want to do with e-mail.** There are numerous purposes that e-mail can serve, and you need to ensure that the purpose is always clear to your trainees. If they know *what* it is being used for, and *why* e-mail has been chosen for this, they are much more likely to get more out of it.

9   **Make the most of e-mail.** Although you may just want to use e-mail for routine communication with (and between) trainees, there are many more uses that the medium can lend itself to. Think about the possible uses of sending attached files, such as documents, assignments, digitally stored images, sounds and video recordings. All of these can be edited or marked, and returned to trainees, in the same ways as simple messages.

10 **Collect your e-mail frequently and reply quickly.** If you don't collect your e-mail frequently and respond promptly, you will lose out on the benefits of fast communications and other people will be less inclined to send you e-mail in future.

11   **Make the most of the lack of time constraints.** One of the most significant advantages of e-mail as a vehicle for feedback is that trainees can view the feedback when they have time to make sense of it. They can store it until such time becomes available. They can also look at it as often as they wish to, and you can keep copies of exactly what you said to each individual trainee.

12   **Be available!** When trainees are accustomed to e-mail, they expect quick replies to their queries. If you're going to be away from your access to the system for more than a day or two at a time, it is worth letting all your trainees know when you will be back on-line.

13   **Make the most of the speed.** Giving feedback by e-mail to trainees at a distance obviously reduces delays. The sooner trainees get feedback on their work, the more likely it is that their own thinking is still fresh in their minds and the feedback is, therefore, better understood.

14   **Keep e-mail messages simple.** Most e-mail systems have very limited editing facilities and can only handle straightforward text. They don't allow different fonts or typestyles and diagrams are not possible, so messages tend not to look attractive. The reason for this is to let a very wide variety of systems communicate in a very simple way.

15   **Make most messages really brief and to the point.** Few people take much notice of long e-mail messages. If something takes more than one screen, most readers either dump them or file them. Encourage your trainees also to make good use of the medium, and to send several short messages rather than try to cram lots of points into a single missive.

16   **When you send a long e-mail, explain why, and what to do with it.** For example, from time to time you may want to send trainees something that you don't expect them to treat as a normal e-mail message, but perhaps to print out and study in depth. It makes all the difference if they know what they are expected to do with longer messages.

17   **Send more detailed messages as attached files.** If you want to send more detailed communications, you can produce them in another, more flexible computer package. If you save the file you produce, you can then send this with a short e-mail message explaining what you are sending.

18   **Make sure the recipient has software to read attached files.** If you send a complex file such as a word processed document or a spreadsheet, make sure the recipient can read them. Ideally they would have the same version of the program that you used to create it, but it may be possible to send a file which is saved in a format compatible with the recipient's software, even if it isn't the same.

19 **Make use of mailing lists to send copies to more than one recipient at the same time.** Most e-mail software makes it very simple to send extra copies of a message to other people. It is also often possible to create lists, or groups, of people and to send messages to all the members of the groups at the same time. These groups can also be saved for future mailings.

20 **Encourage trainees to reply about your feedback.** When you are using e-mail to give specific feedback to trainees, it is important that you know that you have got through to them all. Asking them to reply to you gives them the chance to let you know how they *feel* about the feedback you have given them, or the mark or grade that you have awarded them.

21 **Use e-mail to keep a dispersed or distant group of trainees together.** Sending out circular notes not only helps individuals to feel part of a community of trainees, but also reminds them about important matters such as assessment deadlines, or problems that have arisen with course materials, or updates to interesting materials that have been discovered on the Internet.

22 **Remember those trainees whose access to e-mail is difficult or impossible.** One of the disadvantages of using e-mail as a means of communication on training programmes is that if some trainees have problems with access, they can become significantly disadvantaged. You may need to find ways of compensating through other means for those things they miss out on.

23 **Take particular care with your e-mail message titles.** It can take ages to search for a particular e-mail if it is not clear what each message is about. The computer software can sort messages by date, and by sender, but it is more difficult to track down topics. Two or three well chosen keywords make the most useful titles.

35

Helping trainees to get started with e-mail

The use of electronic mail has accelerated rapidly in the last few years. We've already explored how *you* can get started with e-mail, and next we look at ways you can help your trainees to take the plunge. People who would not have been thought to be computer literate often take their first steps into the area because they are attracted by the benefits of e-mail. Some, perhaps many, of your trainees are likely to be up to speed with computers and e-mail, but the following suggestions may help you to whet the appetites of those who have not yet become 'mouse-trained'.

1   **Mention how unlikely it is that trainees will break the computer!** For those trainees who are reluctant to get into computer usage, there is often a concern that they may do something drastic and irreversible to expensive equipment. Remind trainees that the only thing they are likely to risk when using computers is losing some of the work they have done with the machine, and even this risk is quite small with 'undo' commands in most computer software, and with good habits about saving work to disk every few minutes.

2   **Point out that e-mail is a way of practising useful written communication skills.** Getting trainees to communicate with each other, and with you, using e-mail helps them to develop their written command of the language. Seeing their own words on-screen rather than on paper can make them more aware of their strengths and weaknesses with the language.

3   **Promote the benefits of computer literacy.** The information technology revolution has meant that a much greater proportion of people need to use computers in their everyday work and lives. Being computer literate also means that people don't have to rely on other people to perform

various tasks for them. For example, trainees who have mastered word processing don't have to pay someone to process their reports or memos, and can keep editorial control over them, making it much easier to change them whenever they receive some useful feedback about draft versions.

4   **Remind trainees that an e-mail message need not be sent until they are completely happy with it.** This allows them to edit and polish their writing. If they were to attempt so much editing on a handwritten message, it could either look very messy, or have to be written out several times, before the same amount of adjustment had been achieved.

5   **Remind trainees that e-mail can be viewed as environment-friendly.** The saving of paper can be significant. If the computing facilities are already available, it can be argued that using e-mail incurs negligible costs.

6   **Point out to trainees that they can save and keep their own e-mail communications.** By copying each e-mailed message to their own files or disks, they can keep track of all the messages they have composed and sent. Keeping similar track of handwritten messages is less likely, or would involve the trouble and expense of photocopying. Trainees, looking back at a range of e-mails they have composed, can see for themselves how their skills with the language are developing.

7   **Remind trainees that e-mail can be a way of them keeping in touch with their friends elsewhere.** Most libraries or colleges have Internet facilities available to trainees, making it possible for them to send messages to anywhere in the world. Such facilities are sometimes free of charge to library users, and in any case the actual costs are insignificant once the equipment has been installed.

8   **Help trainees to get started.** Probably the best way to do this is for you to *require* all of your trainees to e-mail something short to you, with a time deadline. It can be worth thinking about using a short written exercise for this purpose, in which case you can attach at least some marks to the task. This can make all the difference to trainees who might otherwise not get round to finding out how to log into the system and send an e-mail.

9   **Make trainees' efforts worthwhile.** If you've asked all members of a group to e-mail something to you, try to respond *immediately* (within a day or two) to each message as it arrives. The fact that trainees get a little individual feedback via e-mail from you, and quickly, helps them to see for themselves the potential of e-mail as a communication medium.

10   **Encourage trainees to write very short e-mails!** One of the problems with e-mail communication is that people only tend to read the beginning of a message. If an incoming message is too long for immediate reading, people tend either to file them away for later reading (and forget them!) or simply delete them.

36

Giving trainees feedback using e-mail and computer conferencing

Computer communications are very fast and cheap, so they are very useful for providing feedback to trainees. Once you have established a culture of using computer communications for aspects of your training, develop its use for feedback as well. E-mail is particularly useful as a vehicle for giving trainees individual feedback on assessed work, whether as stand alone e-mail communications to trainees, or alongside or within a computer conferencing system. Electronic feedback can apply to computer-mediated coursework (where the work is submitted through a computer system), but can also extend usefully to giving trainees feedback on handwritten or hard copy work that they have submitted for assessment. The following suggestions may help you to exploit the benefits of e-mail, not least to save you time and energy in giving trainees feedback.

1   **Encourage trainees to send you assessments or samples of work as e-mail attachments.** If work is being produced on a computer, it is easy and quick to attach a saved file to an e-mail message. It will arrive very quickly and it is very cheap to send it.

2   **Make the most of the comfort of privacy.** When trainees receive feedback by e-mail (as opposed to face to face or in group situations), they have the comfort of being able to read the feedback without anyone (particularly you!) being able to see their reactions to it. This is most useful when you need to give some critical feedback to trainees.

3   **Remember that you can edit your own feedback before you send it.** For example, you may well want to adjust individual feedback comments in the light of trainees' overall performance. It is much harder to edit handwritten feedback on trainees' written work. E-mail feedback allows you to type in immediate feedback to things that you see in each trainee's work, and to adjust or delete particular parts of your feedback as you go further into marking their work.

4   **Exploit the space.** Inserting handwritten feedback comments into trainees' written work is limited by the amount of space that there may be for your comments. With e-mail feedback, you don't have to restrict your wording if you need to elaborate on a point.

5   **Acknowledge receipt of assessments.** Trainees will be worried that their work hasn't arrived safely, so tell them when it has arrived. An e-mail message is best for this because it is private.

6   **Provide specific feedback to individuals by e-mail.** As this method of communication is private, it is suitable for giving comments on work to individuals. It is much easier to write this kind of communication by computer than by hand, so use the technology for the whole process.

7   **Investigate word processing software to help with assessment of written work.** If work is produced by word processing, it is often possible to add comments to it. You can use this to provide comments on the work as part of the feedback process.

8   **Consider combining e-mail feedback with written feedback.** For example, you can write on to trainees' work a series of numbers or letters, at the points where you wish to give detailed feedback. The e-mail feedback can then translate these numbers or letters into feedback comments or phrases, so that trainees can see exactly what each element of feedback is telling them. The fact that trainees then have to decode each feedback element helps them to think about it more deeply, and learn from it more effectively, than when they can see the feedback directly on their work.

9   **Spare yourself from repeated typing.** When designing computer-delivered feedback messages, you should only have to type each message once. You can then copy and paste all of the messages where you need to give several trainees the same feedback information. It can be useful to combine this process with numbers or letters, which you write onto trainees' work, and building up each e-mail to individual trainees by pasting together the feedback messages which go with each of the numbers or letters.

10   **Consider the possibilities of 'global' feedback messages.** For example, you may wish to give all of the trainees in a large group the same feedback message about overall matters arising from a test or exercise. The overall message can be pasted into each e-mail, before the individual comments addressed to each trainee.

11   **Check that your e-mail feedback is getting through.** Most e-mail systems can be programmed to send you back a message saying when the e-mail was opened, and by whom. This can help you to identify any trainees who are not opening their e-mails. It can also be useful to end each e-mail with a question, asking the trainee to reply to you on some point arising from the feedback. This helps to make sure that trainees don't just open their e-mail feedback messages, but have to read them!

12   **Keep records of your e-mail feedback.** It is easy to keep copies on disk of all of your feedback to each trainee, and you can open a folder for each trainee if you wish. This makes it much easier to keep track of your ongoing feedback to individual trainees, than when your handwritten feedback is lost to you when you return their work to them.

13   **Make the most of the technology.** For example, many e-mail systems support spellcheck facilities, which can allow you to type really fast and ignore most of the resulting errors, until you correct them all just before sending your message. This also causes you to reread each message, which can be very useful for encouraging you to add second thoughts, which may have occurred to you as you went further in your assessment of the task.

14   **Use e-mail to gather feedback from your trainees.** Trainees are often bolder sitting at a computer terminal than they are face to face. Ask your trainees questions about how they are finding selected aspects of their studies, but don't turn it into an obvious routine questionnaire. Include some open-ended questions, so that they feel free to let you know how they are feeling about their own progress, and about your teaching too.

15   **Use a computer conference to provide subtle pressure on trainees to submit work on time.** Publish lists of work you have received from trainees, but without names. This will make those who haven't submitted work realize that they could be falling behind.

16   **Create a new conference topic for discussion of each assessment.** Trainees may want to exchange ideas after they have received feedback on assessed work. If you provide a topic for this, they will know where to discuss this without affecting the structure of the rest of the conference.

17   **Seek permission from participants to use their work to give general feedback to the group.** If the work of one of the trainees includes something that you could use to illustrate a useful point to the whole group, ask their permission to use it. An e-mail message is the appropriate medium to use for this, and the work could remain anonymous. Once you have permission, you can copy the appropriate sections to the conference and discuss it there.

18   **Use the conference system to provide general feedback to groups.** When assessing work, there will be common points that need to be raised for several people. If these are discussed on the group's conference without naming anybody, participants can learn from each other's mistakes.

19   **Consider putting assessment statistics on the conference.** You could make some basic information (such as average scores) available to the group. Some people might find it helpful to see how their performance compared with others in the group. On the other hand, some people might find this demoralizing, so this issue needs careful thought.

37

Thinking about using computer conferencing for training

There are several parallel names for this, including computer-mediated communication (CMC), computer-supported cooperative learning and, more simply, on-line learning. Whatever we call them, computer conferences can be of great value in training programmes, especially where the trainees are geographically dispersed, but working on similar timescales. Many of the suggestions made about e-mail continue to apply, but in this section we would like to alert you to some of the additional factors to consider with computer conferences. Computer conferences are very similar to e-mail, but the messages are sent to all the people who are members of a conference. Conferences allow groups to discuss ideas together and, if the Internet is used, members can be anywhere in the world. The person who runs the conference is called the moderator. The moderator has control over who is a member of the conference and can set up sub-conferences (or topics). This person can also delete messages and so has some editorial control over the conference. The following suggestions may help you to plan whether to use computer conferencing, and point you towards maximizing the benefits that your trainees can derive from computer conferencing.

1   **Note the differences between computer conferencing and other forms of electronic communication.** The distinguishing feature of computer conferencing is that many people can see the same contents, from different places, and at any time. The contents 'grow' as further notes and replies are added by participants. Most systems automatically alert participants to 'new messages' that have been added since they last viewed the conference, and allow these messages to be read first if desired.

2 **Regard computer conferences as virtual classrooms, seminar rooms and libraries.** Computer conferences can be each of these. They can provide a virtual classroom, where the whole trainee group can 'meet'. They can be used to provide a virtual seminar room, closed to all but a small learning group of around six trainees. They can function as virtual libraries, where resource banks and materials are kept. They can also function as trainee only gossip areas. Each of these ways of using computer conferences can emulate electronically the related best practice in face-to-face training environments.

3 **Work out definite purposes for each computer conference.** Conferences are much more successful when they are provided to relate to identified needs, or specific intended outcomes. It is worth working out how best you may use computer conferencing with your own trainees well before starting one up.

4 **Get involved in computer-conferencing situations yourself first.** If you have access to e-mail or the Internet, one of the best ways to pave the way towards putting computer conferencing to good use with your trainees is to participate yourself. For example, join some discussion lists, and experience at first hand the things that work and the things that go wrong with such means of communication.

5 **Explore the computer conferencing systems from which you can choose.** There are several systems available around the world, each with their own formats, features and idiosyncrasies. If most of your trainees are not particularly computer literate, go for a system that makes it as easy as possible to log on and to add messages.

6 **Investigate what computer conferencing facilities your organization has available.** If there is already a mechanism for computer conferencing, it makes sense to see if you can use that, rather than starting from scratch on your own. You may also be able to tap into existing expertise that exists in your organization.

7 **Carefully evaluate computer conferencing facilities offered by other organizations.** There will be a range of companies who are keen to sell you facilities based on their computer systems. You will need to investigate them thoroughly to make sure that you choose the best systems for your needs.

8 **Question potential conference providers thoroughly.** Find out about prices for setting up the conference and for providing space for storing messages: is there a limit on message storage and how much does it cost

to buy more? Check the software that the systems use: which is the easiest to use, and are essential facilities included? Are good help facilities provided in case you have problems setting up conferences? If conference members will be connecting to the system by modem, are there plenty of telephone access points to the system so that calls are charged at local rates? Also check that the modems at these telephone access points are reasonably fast.

9   **Make sure that conference members have good help provision.** Ordinary conference members do not need help with setting up or moderating conferences as they will use the ones you set up. Make sure that any manuals or help facilities are correctly targeted to provide an appropriate level of support for ordinary conference users.

10   **Check up on the levels of security and privacy provided.** It is important that conference members are happy that their messages can only be read by the intended audience. It may also be useful to enable sub groups within the conference to communicate privately from the main conference.

11   **Find out about the e-mail facilities offered by the conference providers.** E-mail is a very useful addition to conferences as it enables private messages to be sent to individuals. The ability to communicate separately from the conference can be very helpful.

12   **Make sure that all of your trainees will be able to access all the conferences which you want them to.** Ideally, you may also intend them to be able to download and/or print chosen extracts from the conference for their own personal study purposes. You can only build a computer conference into a training programme as an essential component if all of your trainees are able to participate. If the conference is just an optional extra for those able to join it, other trainees who can't may be able to claim to have been disadvantaged.

13   **Try to practise setting up and moderating conferences before the real one starts.** A few colleagues may be willing to take part in a pilot exercise so that you can develop your skills by practising on them. Start this well in advance of your first real conference so that you can overcome problems and gain confidence.

14   **Make sure that trainees will have sufficient access to networked terminals.** In particular, if contribution to a computer conference may be linked in any way to assessment, it is essential to ensure that trainees cannot appeal against assessment decisions on the grounds of not being able to contribute due to lack of opportunity.

38

Getting a computer conference going

The success of a computer conference depends upon its value to trainees, and how well they can make good use of it. This, in turn, depends significantly on the design and structure of the conference, and on the degree of ownership they develop about it. The following suggestions may help you to tread sensitively regarding moderating a conference, while setting it up so as to maximize its value to trainees.

1   **Explain to trainees the benefits of participating in computer conferences.** Trainees can exchange a lot of information, both study related and social, through such conferences. They can get peer feedback on their own ideas, and even on selected parts of their work. Participating in computer conferences helps trainees to develop computer related skills, and can quickly help them to speed up their keyboarding skills.

2   **Provide good 'start-up' pages.** These are the initial notes, to which trainees can append their replies. Each 'start-up' page should have a definite purpose, so that replies and ensuing discussion is focused rather than rambling. These are essentially the main topics of the conference, and are listed sequentially in the main directory of the conference. Conferencing takes place when participants add 'replies' to these pages. The replies are normally listed in the sub directory of each start-up page in the order in which they are received.

3   **Make each screen speak for itself.** Especially with 'start-up' pages, which introduce each topic in the conference, it is best that the essence of the main message takes up less than a single screen. Further detail can be added in the next few pages (or 'replies'). Encourage trainees contributing their own replies to keep them to a single screen whenever possible, and to send several replies with different titles rather than one long reply addressing a number of different aspects.

4   **Aim to get the essence of a 'start-up' page on to a single screen of information or less.** If trainees have to scroll down more than one page before finding out what is being addressed, they are less likely to read the 'start-up' page, and therefore unlikely to reply.

5   **Choose the titles of 'start-up' pages carefully.** When trainees are looking at the directory of a computer conference, they will see the titles of these pages arranged as an index, in the order in which the pages were originally entered. Aim to make these titles self-explanatory, so that trainees can tell what each section of the conference is about directly from the directory, rather than having to read the whole of a 'start-up' page before finding out whether they wish to explore the topic further.

6   **Don't cover too much in a 'start-up' page.** It is better if each section of the conference is relatively self-contained, and prescribed, rather than having topic pages which cover several different aspects. As new matters arise from trainees' replies to 'start-up' pages, decide whether to introduce new 'start-up' pages to carry these matters forward separately. Add your own responses which will direct trainees, who may be following the conference theme, to where in the conference each theme is being developed further.

7   **Choose the topics within your conference carefully.** Think about the structure you want the conference to take and set up a topic for each main area. Topics that are too general may end up with messages that are not clearly focused and discussions may not develop well.

8   **Start with a small number of topics and only add more when they are needed.** It is confusing to have too many topics at first, so only have a few at the beginning. As the training develops and new subjects become relevant to your trainees, add new conference topics to provide discussion areas.

9   **Make sure messages are put into the correct topic.** If messages are put into the wrong topic, the structure of the discussions will suffer. Encourage conference members to think about where to put messages at a very early stage, and try to establish a culture of well organized discussion. If some members consistently place messages in the wrong place, send them an e-mail explaining what they have done and what would be better. If they persist in doing this, you may need to use your moderating powers to move messages to the correct place.

10 **Encourage trainees to reply with messages that are short and only contain one point.** Long messages are difficult to read on computer screens, so discourage any that are more than one screen long. If messages contain discussion of more than one point, the structure of the conference can break down, so encourage members to send several short messages, addressing one point each.

11 **Leave a message every time you log on.** One of the concerns that computer conference users have is that nobody is reading their messages. Use the conference as frequently as you can, and always leave some kind of message to show that you have been logging in. Ideally your messages should answer questions or raise some important issue, but a trivial message in the 'chat' topic is better than nothing.

12 **Use the conference as a notice board.** Get into the habit of making the conference *the* best way to keep up with topical developments in the field of study, as well as administrative matters such as assessment deadlines, guidance for trainees preparing assessments, and so on. Try to make it necessary for trainees to log on to the conference regularly; this will result in a greater extent of active contribution by them. A conference can provide you with a quick and efficient way to communicate detailed information to the whole class. Trainees themselves can print off and keep anything that is particularly important to them.

13 **Use the conference as a support mechanism.** This can save a lot of tutor time. Elements of explanation, advice or counselling that otherwise may have had to be sent individually to several different trainees can be put into the conference once only, and remain available to all. Whenever your reply to an enquiry or problem raised by a trainee warrants a wider audience, the conference is there to do this.

14 **Make the conference a resource in its own right.** Add some screens of useful resource material, maybe with 'hot links' to other Internet sources that are relevant. It is useful if some such material is *only* available through the computer conference; this ensures that all your trainees will make efforts to use it.

15 **Try to get trainees discussing and arguing with each other via the conference.** The best computer conferences are not just tutor–trainee debates, but are taken over by the trainees themselves. They can add new topics, and bring a social dimension to the conference.

16 **Set up a 'chat' topic for general conversation.** Conference members might want to discuss matters that are less serious than the training aspects of the conference. Set up an area for them to do this and encourage them to 'chat' in that area. Other names for 'chat' conferences might be 'café' or 'pub': choose a name to suit the tone you are trying to establish for your conference.

17 **Encourage members to use e-mail where it is more appropriate.** E-mail is more private, and so it should be used for messages that are for individuals rather than for general distribution to all conference members. There is also no point in making others read messages which are not relevant to them.

18 **Try to moderate with a light hand.** If people are putting messages in the wrong topic, or are not using e-mail appropriately, provide gentle guidance about what to do in future. As far as you can, keep the ownership of the content and structure of the conference with the participants themselves, rather than being tempted into editing the conference too much.

19 **Be prepared to moderate rigorously if necessary!** For example, remove anything offensive or inappropriate before it is likely to be seen by many trainees. If particular trainees misuse the conference, treat the issue seriously, and seek them out and warn them of the consequences of such actions, for example, loss of computer privileges. It is useful to recruit trainee moderators from those trainees who are particularly computer literate, and who may be only too willing to become conference moderators, editing and rearranging contributions to keep the structure of the conference fluent and easy to follow.

20 **Consider having some assessed work entered on to the conference.** If trainees *have to* make some contributions, they are more likely to ascend the learning curve in regard to sending in replies, and to do so more readily in non-assessed elements, too. One advantage in having an assessed task 'up on the conference' is that each trainee can see everyone else's attempts, and the standards of work improve very rapidly.

21 **Consider allocating some of the coursework marks for participation in a computer conference.** This is one way of ensuring that all the trainees in a class engage with a class-conference. Once they have mastered the technique of contributing to a conference, most trainees find that they enjoy it enough to maintain a healthy level of participation.

39

Using the Internet for training

Trainees may be able to use the Internet at times of their own choice, in their own ways, at their own pace, and from anywhere that access to it is available to them. That said, this does not mean that it is automatically a vehicle for productive and effective learning. Indeed, it is very easy to become sidetracked by all sorts of fascinating things, and to stray well away from any intended learning outcome. The suggestions which follow are not intended as starting points for setting out to *deliver* training through the Internet, but rather to help trainees to *use* the Internet to obtain material to use in connection with their studies, such as in assignments they are preparing. The following suggestions may help you to help your trainees both to enjoy the Internet *and* to learn well from it.

1   **Play with the Internet yourself.** You need to pick up your own experience of how it feels to tap into such a vast and varied database, before you can design ways of delivering it to your trainees with some meaningful learning experiences.

2   **Decide whether you want your trainees to use the Internet, or an Intranet.** An Intranet is where a networked set of computers talk to each other, whilst using Internet conventions, but where the content is not open to the rest of the universe. If you are working in an organization which already has such a network, and if your trainees can make use of this network effectively, there will be some purposes that will be better served by an Intranet. You can also have *controlled* access to the Internet via an Intranet, such as by using hot links to predetermined external sites.

3   **Use the Internet to research something yourself.** You may well, of course, have done this often already but, if not, give it a try before you think of setting your trainees 'search and retrieve' tasks with the Internet. Set yourself a fixed time, perhaps half an hour or even less. Choose a topic that you're going to search for, preferably something a little offbeat. See for yourself how best to use the search engines, and compare the efficiency of different engines. Find out for yourself how to deal with 4593 references

to your chosen topic, and how to improve your searching strategy to whittle them down to the ten that you really want to use!

4 **Don't just use the Internet as a filing cabinet for your own training resources!** While it is useful in its own way if your trainees can have access to your own notes and resources, this is not really *using* the Internet. Too many materials designed for use in other forms are already cluttering up the Internet. If all you intend your trainees to do is to download your notes and print their own copies, sending them e-mailed attachments would do the same job much more efficiently.

5 **Think carefully about your intended training outcomes.** You may indeed wish to use the Internet as a means whereby your trainees address the existing intended outcomes associated with their subject material. However, it is also worth considering whether you may wish to add further training outcomes to do with the processes of searching, selecting, retrieving and analyzing subject material. If so, you may also need to think about whether, and how, these additional training outcomes may be assessed.

6 **Give your trainees specific things to do by using the Internet.** Make these tasks, where it is relevant, have up-to-the-minute data or news, instead of tasks where the 'answers' are already encapsulated in easily accessible books or training resources.

7 **Consider giving your trainees a menu of tasks and activities.** They will feel more ownership if they have a significant degree of choice in their Internet tasks. Where you have a group of trainees working on the same syllabus, it can be worth letting them choose different tasks, and then communicating their main findings to each other (and to you), using a computer conference or by e-mail.

8 **Let your trainees know that the process is at least as important as the outcome.** The key skills that they can develop using the Internet include designing an effective search, and making decisions about the quality and authenticity of the evidence they find. It is worth designing tasks where you already know of at least some of the evidence you expect them to locate, and remaining open to the fact that they will each uncover at least as much again as you already know about!

9 **Consider designing your own interactive pages.** You may want to restrict these to an Intranet, at least at first. You can then use dialogue boxes to encourage your trainees to answer questions, enter data, and so on. Putting such pages up for all to see on the Internet may mean that you get a lot of unsolicited replies!

10   **Consider getting your trainees to design and enter some pages.** This may be best done restricted to an Intranet, at least until your trainees have picked up sufficient skills to develop pages that are worth putting up for all to see. The act of designing their own Internet material is one of the most productive ways to help your trainees develop their critical skills at evaluating materials already on the Internet.

40

Information retrieval from the Internet

The Internet has enormous potential as a source of information for a vast range of tasks. It can also, however, lead to problems and it needs to be used with care. Passing some of this guidance on to trainees will help them avoid pitfalls.

1   **Choose your times carefully.** If you plan to give trainees information retrieval tasks using the Internet during course time, make sure that you organize this so that the system will not be too congested at the time. When the system is busy, it becomes very slow and communications can even break down. If possible, use it when the USA is asleep (in the mornings for UK users).

2   **Think about the time it might take and what the costs might be for your trainees to find information.** The Internet is generally cheap to use, but costs can mount up. If trainees are using a modem to make their connection, encourage them to do it at weekends or in the evenings to reduce costs. Make sure they have the opportunity to search at these times. You might need to give trainees some hints about where they should search, so that they don't waste too much time.

3   **Use 'local' sources when possible.** A number of organizations have sites in different parts of the world. If you can find one in the same country (or even continent) that you are working from, communications can be faster at busy times.

4   **Use a good search engine to help you find information.** There are quite a few search engines available on the Internet. Choose one that seems to perform quickly and that produces a good range of results. Once again, some search engines have sites in different parts of the world, so using a 'local' one may be faster.

5   **Learn to use the advanced facilities of a search engine to refine searches.**
Simple searches on almost any single word produce too many matches to
be useful. Search engines usually allow you to carry out more refined
searches in order to home in more accurately on the information you are
looking for. Many of these engines include tutorials that will help you to
use them effectively.

6   **Be prepared to use the rest of the Internet, as well as the World Wide
Web.** Most Internet users are familiar with the graphical user interface of
the World Wide Web (WWW). This is the easiest part of the Internet to
use, but some of the other parts make a wider range of information
available and (because they don't use graphics widely) are much faster in
operation. If the WWW doesn't have the information you need, try to
find out about using FTP (File Transfer Protocol), Gopher servers and
Veronicas. They may seem difficult to use, but they give access to a wide
range of information.

7   **Be cautious about the quality of the information available on the
Internet.** It is very cheap and easy to set up pages, particularly on the
WWW. As a result, the quality of the information is very variable. Before
relying on it, check out the reliability of the source of the information.
The information could have been put there by students as a prank, by a
fundamentalist group or by a company for sales purposes. Ideally, you
should only use information that provides some means (such as references)
for verifying it.

8   **Insist that trainees acknowledge their sources of information.** If a source
is used, trainees should give the address of the page where it was found.
This enables the source to be verified and discourages plagiarism.

9   **Be aware that information on the Internet can change or be moved.** It is
quite common for links from one page to another page, or another site, to
change. A page can also be moved to a different server. Before directing
trainees to a source of information, make sure it is still there.

10   **Make sure trainees don't drift around on the surf.** It is very easy to follow
interesting links around the Internet and to spend a lot of time
unproductively. Warn your trainees against this danger and give them
some idea how much time should be spent on Internet tasks.

41

Helping trainees to learn from the Internet

The Internet is the electronic highway to the largest collection of information, data and communication ever constructed by the human species. There is information available through the WWW on every imaginable subject. Playing with the Internet is easy, but *learning* from it is not always straightforward. The following suggestions may help you to point your trainees in directions where they will not only enjoy playing with the Internet, but also develop their techniques so that they learn effectively from it, too.

1   **Consider starting small.** For example, you might be able to download selected information from the Internet on to individual computers, or a locally networked series of terminals. You can then give your trainees specific 'search' tasks, where it will be relatively easy for them to locate specific information.

2   **Get your trainees to induct each other.** Learning from the Internet need not be a solo activity. Indeed, it can be very useful to have two or three trainees working at each terminal, so that they talk to each other about what they are finding, and follow up leads together. Encourage them to take turns at working the keyboard, so that they all develop their confidence at handling the medium, and are then equipped to carry on working on their own.

3   **Give your trainees exercises that help them to improve their selection of search words.** Show them how choosing a single broad search word leads to far too many sources being listed, and makes it very slow and boring to go through all of the sources looking for the information they are really wanting. Get them to experiment with different combinations of search words, so that the sources that are located become much more relevant to their search purposes.

4   **Allow your trainees to find out about the different speeds at which information can be found on the Internet.** For example, let them experiment at different times of the day, so they can see when the Internet is heavily used and slower. Also let them find out for themselves how much slower it can be waiting for graphics to be downloaded than for mainly text materials. Help them to become better at deciding whether to persist with a source that is highly relevant but slow to download, or whether to continue searching for sources which may download more quickly.

5   **Remind your trainees that finding information is only the first step in learning from it.** It is easy to discover a wealth of information during an Internet search, only to forget most of it within a very short time. Encourage your trainees to download and edit the materials that they think will be most relevant, or even to make conventional handwritten or word processed notes of their own while they use the Internet.

6   **Help your trainees to learn to keep tabs on what they have found.** Entering 'bookmarks' or 'favourites' is one of the most efficient ways of being able to go back easily to what may have turned out to be the most relevant or valuable source of information during a search. Get your trainees to practise logging the sites that could turn out to be worth returning to. Also help them to practise clearing out bookmarks that turn out to be irrelevant, or that are superseded by later finds.

7   **Give your trainees practice at recording things that they have found during searches.** It can be useful to design worksheets to train them to note down key items of information as they find it, and to train them to be better at making their own notes as a matter of routine when exploring a topic using the Internet.

8   **Consider getting your trainees to keep a learning log.** This can be done for a few hours of work with the Internet, and then looked back upon for clues about which tactics proved most successful. It can be even better to get trainees to compare notes about what worked well for them, and where the glitches were.

9   **Help your trainees to develop their critical skills.** For example, set them a task involving them reviewing several sources they find on the Internet, and making decisions about the authenticity and validity of the information that they locate. Remind them that it is not possible to tell whether information is good or bad just by looking at the apparent quality of it on the screen. Remind your trainees that information on the Internet may not have been subjected to refereeing or other quality assurance processes normally associated with published information in books or journal articles.

10 **Remind trainees to balance playing with the Internet and learning from it.** It is perfectly natural, and healthy, to explore, and to follow up interesting leads, even when they take trainees far away from the purpose of their searches. However, it is useful to develop the skills to ration the amount of random exploration, and to devote 'spurts' of conscious activity to following through the specific purposes of searches.

Chapter 6   Computer-delivered Assessment and Evaluation

Our final chapter in this book is about a more specific agenda than much of the rest of the book: assessment of trainees' work, and the use of computers in such assessment. If your work with trainees does not involve such assessment, you may not wish to use this chapter at all. However, we would encourage you to scan it, as using computers may provide you with ways of reducing your own workload in due course.

Computer-delivered tests can save trainers from tiresome, routine marking. They can also be really useful for trainees themselves, who can get instant feedback (if you choose to give them this) from the computer as they work through computer-delivered tests. Designing such tests is time intensive, but when the number of trainees who will use the tests is high, it becomes a wise investment of your time.

Computer-mediated coursework is being used increasingly in higher and further education, and its benefits extend to training, too.

We have already offered many suggestions in this book about computer-generated feedback, so we include only a summary of the main considerations in this chapter about assessment.

We end the chapter by looking at the other side of assessment: evaluation by trainees of their training experience. Once again, using computers to collect and analyze feedback *from* trainees can save a great deal of time and work. Also, it is found that trainees may prefer to give us feedback through computer-managed questionnaires, rather than filling in yet more handwritten questionnaires.

42

Devising computer-delivered tests for trainees

There are many advantages to using computer-delivered tests, not least of which are that most people actually prefer doing such tests to doing written tests. Computer-marked assignments can save human toil, and can be a means of giving much quicker feedback to trainees than from human trainers. The following suggestions may help you to decide when and how to use computer-marked assignments with your trainees.

1   **Play with some computer-delivered tests yourself.** There is no better way of finding out what computer-delivered tests can do well than to explore how other people have already designed them. There are many examples of structured questions in published computer-marked assignments, and on the Internet. Seeing what other people have already done is the fastest way of working out what sorts of questions you could design for your own purposes. It is also useful for you to find out what it feels like to sit at a terminal and enter in choices to structured questions. Looking at other people's tests is also the best way of finding out what *not* to do in your own work.

2   **Decide whether you are designing *computer-delivered* assignments, or just *computer-marked* ones.** *Computer-marked* assignments can be in print, with, for example, optical card readers used to automate the marking, the printout of feedback to trainees, and the analysis of their scores and the performance of the questions as testing devices. *Computer-delivered* assignments are where trainees enter their answers or choices directly in to a computer or terminal, and may then get feedback and/or scores straightaway from the machine, or across the Internet or an Intranet.

3   **Decide whether you will be using computer-delivered testing for assessment or for feedback – or for both.** With computer-delivered testing formats, you can provide feedback immediately to trainees every time they enter a decision into the machine. Alternatively, you can give them on-screen feedback at the end of the test, for example to those questions that they did not answer correctly. You may also have the option of getting the computer to print out a feedback response that your trainees can take away after the test, reminding them of what they got right as well as what they got wrong in the test.

4   **You don't have to use scores.** It is perfectly valid to use computer-delivered tests purely as a learning device, especially to help trainees to find out for themselves, in the comfort of privacy, what they already know well and where their weaknesses lie. It is normally possible to switch off the scoring element of the software, and simply use each structured question to provide feedback to trainees on the options they choose for each question.

5   **Explore the software options open to you.** There are several different software shells which support testing and feedback delivery. Which you choose will depend on how sophisticated your question design will be, and to some extent how easily you yourself can learn to handle the software. Alternatively, your responsibility may rest mainly in the area of designing questions and feedback, with someone else handling the task of entering your assignments into the software.

6   **Don't become trapped into the belief that computer-marked assignments can only test lower cognitive knowledge.** Although such assignments are often used to test straightforward recall of information or simple decision making, well designed assignments can test at a much deeper level. Look at the different things that can be tested, and the different question structures that are possible. Besides multiple-choice questions, computer-delivered assignments can be designed to use number entry, text entry, ranking and a variety of other ways for trainees to enter their answers or decisions.

7   **Look through your syllabus, and decide what lends itself to computer-delivered testing.** For example, such testing is particularly good for assessing the trainees' grasp of a wide range of information, and whether they have reached a level where they can make correct decisions when presented with a number of options. Computer-delivered testing can interrogate trainees about the best descriptions or definitions of terms and concepts. Such assessment is possible where it is straightforward to design structured questions, particularly multiple-choice ones. This requires there to be a correct (or best) option (referred to as the key), and other incorrect (or less good) options called distractors.

8   **Think about computer literacy implications.** If the assignment is print-based, and only the *marking* is to be done using computers, there is little to worry about, other than to make sure that the instructions regarding how to fill in the optically readable card or sheet are clear and straightforward. If, however, doing the assignment depends on sitting at a computer or terminal and interacting with it, trainees with highly developed keyboarding skills may be advantaged, as may those who have no fear of working with computers.

9   **Look at the exercises that you already use with trainees.** Many of the written exercises will contain elements which lend themselves to computer-delivered assessment. It is particularly useful to consider packaging up straightforward questions which you often use, to save you time (and boredom) in marking trainees' answers by hand.

10   **Look at the most common mistakes made by trainees in existing tests or exercises.** It is often possible to turn these mistakes into distractors in computer-delivered multiple-choice tests. This means that you have the chance to allow trainees to make these anticipated mistakes, then use the computer to give them immediate feedback, which is much more effective than when they have to wait to get back tutor-marked work.

11   **Computer-delivered testing makes good use of multiple-choice question formats.** These allow you to design a number of alternative options, one of which follows on correctly from the 'stem' or question, and others of which reflect the most common mistakes that you know trainees are likely to make. You can then design feedback responses, to appear on-screen or to be printed out, for all of the possibilities. *Check carefully that the correct option really* is *correct*. If there is anything at all doubtful about the key, the most able trainees in particular are likely to be thrown by the question. Also check that there is not the possibility of one of the distractors being arguably correct, too.

12   **Don't get too hooked on multiple-choice formats.** While these are particularly amenable to delivering with computers, you can also use text entry, number entry, and 'hot spots' in your question design. These allow you to test your trainees, using questions asking them to enter in words or phrases from the keyboard, or to do calculations on paper then enter in their numerical answers, or to move the on-screen cursor to a particular point on the screen (for example, locating the wrong component in an on-screen circuit diagram in a 'spot the error' question).

13 **Try out each question thoroughly before including it in an assignment.** You may be able to test out your questions with face-to-face groups of trainees, giving you a great deal of useful feedback about whether your questions are really testing them, and about which questions are too hard or too easy. Alternatively, you may be able to trial your questions in computer-based form as part of training materials, and get the software to analyze how each question performs. This helps you to make a better informed decision about which questions are good enough to include in a computer-marked assignment.

14 **Review your questions on the basis of your trials.** What *looks* like a good structured question does not always turn out to work well. If too many trainees are getting a question wrong, it may well be to do with the wording of the question. If too many are getting it right, it could be that the right answer is given away inadvertently in the wording of the question or of the correct option. Computer-delivered testing software can analyze for you the performance of each question, calculating its 'discrimination index' (a measure of how well the particular question is answered by the trainees whose overall performance is best, and how poorly by those who fare worst overall) and the 'facility value' (a measure of whether the question seems to be too hard, too easy, or just right).

15 **Let the computer do the hard work!** Computer-delivered testing software can print out class lists with marks, and can analyze which questions are the sources of most of your trainees' problems, as well as keeping track of the performance of individual trainees doing a series of computer-delivered tests. Marking multiple-choice or structured tests by hand is time consuming and tedious, so let the computer do the boring stuff, and use the time you save to design really useful feedback responses to the test questions.

43

Designing computer-generated feedback for trainees

If you're using computer-delivered assignments, or computer-based learning materials, you should consider the advantages of exploiting the opportunity to give the computer the job of supplying useful feedback straight to the trainees. The following suggestions aim to help you make computer-generated feedback as useful as possible to your trainees.

1   **Don't miss out on the opportunity to couple feedback with assessment.** Whether you are using computer-marked assignments or computer-delivered exams, the technology makes it possible to give each trainee feedback on each choice of option or each keyed in answer.

2   **Respond to trainees' principal questions.** These are, 'Was I right?', and 'If not, *why* not?' It is particularly helpful to take care to respond well to the second of these questions, through the feedback you design for computer-delivered tests or assignments.

3   **Consider the pros and cons of instant feedback.** With computer-delivered exams, for example, it is possible for feedback to be given to trainees immediately after they have attempted each question. The positive feedback they gain when they answer questions successfully may boost their morale and lead to improved exam performance, but the opposite may happen if they happen to get the first few questions wrong.

4   **Consider 'slightly delayed' feedback.** It is useful if trainees can receive feedback while they still remember what they were thinking of when they answered the questions. In computer-delivered exams, feedback can be shown to trainees on-screen *after* they have completed all of the questions, and when it will not have any effect on their scores.

5   **Think how best to give feedback if it is delayed more significantly.** For example, when posting computer-generated feedback printouts to trainees in response to their computer-marked assignments, there will normally be at least several days between trainees answering the questions and receiving feedback. It is then necessary to make sure that trainees are reminded of the context in which they answered each question.

6   **Always remind trainees both of the question and of the options from which they have selected.** It is important, for example, in multiple-choice formats, not only to remind trainees about the context surrounding the correct (or best) option, but also to remind them of the options which were wrong (or less good).

7   **Don't neglect to congratulate trainees who pick the right (or best) option.** They need two things from the feedback you design into the test: confirmation of exactly *what* was correct in the option they chose, and a few words of praise. Computers don't get tired of showing, 'well done', 'absolutely right', 'yes, of course…' and other messages of confirmation on-screen. Take care, however, not to become boring, such as by saying 'well done' *every* time your trainees get something right – there are hundreds of other ways of wording positive feedback.

8   **Take particular care in your feedback responses to trainees who get things wrong.** They need to find out from your feedback response on-screen *why* their own choice of option was not the right one (or the best one). They also need to be reminded about which choice would have been better, or routed back to have another try at the question, so that they can find out for themselves.

9   **Help trainees to consolidate their learning.** When feedback is being provided on-screen, it is particularly helpful to trainees if they can still see the question and the options from which they made their selection, while reading your feedback to the option that they selected.

10   **Consider using a printout of the test, and the feedback.** Most computer-delivered assessment packages can be programmed to provide a printout for each trainee of all of the questions, along with feedback on the options they selected, as well as an overall result, and feedback on their overall performance. It is useful for trainees to have something they can look at again, when they are not at the computer or terminal.

11   **Use technology to write letters to trainees.** Particularly with computer-marked assignments, it is relatively straightforward to wrap up the feedback printed out for each question into a self-sufficient letter, commenting additionally on their overall performance.

12   **Start the feedback on a personal note.** Computers can be programmed to start a letter with, 'Dear Alison...' rather than, 'Dear Mrs Jones'. Most trainees prefer the personal touch, especially when the feedback is coming from a machine. It is, however, important to use familiar names only if you know what your trainees prefer to be called. The start of the letter can then give one of two or three 'openings', each designed for trainees who have respectively scored brilliantly, average, or not so well.

13   **End the feedback letter with useful advice.** The computer can be programmed to search for topic areas where trainees' answers have shown particular strengths or weaknesses, and can offer topic specific praise or suggestions. It is also useful to end a computer-delivered assignment feedback letter with something useful regarding preparation for the next assignment on the programme.

14   **Don't make computer-generated feedback anonymous!** When the name of the trainer who designed the assignment is printed at the end of computer-generated feedback letters, this person is likely to receive quite a few communications from trainees (even if the name was a fictitious one!). Especially if the tone of each feedback response is warm and helpful, trainees don't feel that the feedback was dreamt up by a machine.

15   **Use computer-delivered tests or exercises to gather feedback from trainees.** For example, you can set a few multiple-choice questions to ask trainees what they think about the test or exercise (not scoring such questions of course). You may be surprised to find out how much trainees like the computer-delivered format, particularly if they find your feedback comments helpful and relevant.

44

Devising computer-mediated coursework for trainees

Computer-mediated coursework can be seen as an extension of computer-delivered testing, and can be built on to well piloted tests you have already developed. The following suggestions may help you to decide how best to exploit the potential benefits of computer-mediated coursework.

1 **But what *is* computer-mediated coursework?** Broadly, this is work handed in by your trainees for marking, feedback or assessment, which is not actually handed in, but delivered to you by computer networks by e-mail or via the Internet. Correspondingly, you may give your feedback to trainees by e-mail. Alternatively, you may be in the position of having some computers or terminals already loaded with the coursework tasks, at which trainees enter their own work, which you can later assess at the terminal, or download from the terminal and assess elsewhere.

2 **Don't throw the baby out with the bathwater!** If you have already used coursework in traditional ways, the same agenda is likely to be a good basis for computer-mediated work. The same tasks and exercises which you used to assess trainees' skills, knowledge and competences can be the foundation for computer-based versions.

3 **Work out the benefits for your trainees.** For example, if your trainees are geographically dispersed for considerable periods between training sessions, computer-mediated coursework can be done almost anywhere where there's a computer and a telephone line or mobile phone, and sent to you from anywhere in the country or the world. Such coursework can then be done to schedule by a cohort of trainees working far away from the training centre.

4   **Remind trainees that they can have full control of when they send their work in.** They can enter it on to a computer, save it to floppy disk, edit and polish it several times, until they are quite ready to submit it for assessment. This can reduce the tension associated with coursework, and make it easier for them to continue to adjust it until they are satisfied that they have done their best with it.

5   **Consider building in feedback along the way.** For example, you may find that it saves time both for you and for your trainees if you allocate some of the assessment marks for submission of a plan or an early draft, so that you can give interim feedback to trainees about how their work is shaping up. This can save them going off on tangents, and make their final submissions much more focused and easier to assess.

6   **Use computer-mediated coursework as a basis for communication with your trainees.** The advantages are obvious if your trainees are at a distance for some of the time, but it is still useful to have alternatives to face-to-face communication, even if your trainees are all in the same building. You, and they, can read and respond to each other's comments and feedback in the comfort of privacy.

7   **Think about what's in it for you.** It is easier, for example, to carry around one or two floppy disks containing the work of a number of trainees, than to lug around heavy piles of written papers. It is also very easy to make backup copies of their work, maybe on hard disk, to spare you from the worry of losing some of their coursework.

8   **Remember that a computer is not like a book.** People working with a computer can only see one screen at a time. With a book, people can go backwards and forwards at will, and insert fingers between pages, so that they can make sense of the information on several different pages at once. When setting tasks via a computer screen, you need to make it easy for trainees to see the whole of the task in one eyeful.

9   **Consider giving trainees a printout of the task briefing anyway.** This allows them to look at the task when they're not sitting beside a computer, and increases the chances of them thinking about the task elsewhere.

10   **Introduce computer-mediated coursework a little at a time.** It is useful to get all of your trainees well accustomed to putting their work into a computer before giving them something significant to do in the same way. Computer-mediated coursework should not be testing trainees' competence with the system, but should be assessing their subject-related knowledge or skills.

45

Giving trainees feedback on assessed work

In earlier parts of this book we've made numerous suggestions about ways of ensuring that trainees receive timely, useful feedback on their learning. Feedback is particularly important when trainees' work is being assessed. The following suggestions may remind you of some of the key issues in making sure that trainees derive the maximum benefit from feedback on their assessed work.

1   **Remember that trainees may be quite anxious about feedback on their assessed work.** This has implications for the tone and style that you use to deliver feedback to them. Be particularly careful when providing critical feedback, and don't forget to find something to praise in their work.

2   **Use a word processor for providing written feedback.** Once you are practised at using them, word processors are quicker than handwriting and much less tiring to use. The results should be easier to read than handwriting too.

3   **A 'statement bank' can help you produce feedback quickly.** An extra benefit of word processing is that it is easy to copy and paste text. This has great benefits if you are providing feedback to a large number of trainees. It is common to find that several people have made the same mistake or need similar comments on parts of their work, and you can copy comments from one person's feedback to another's.

4   **You can print each page of a multi-part feedback form individually.** Handwriting on a form that produces several copies is hard work, as considerable pressure is needed to copy the text to all the parts. It is easy to separate the parts and print them individually.

5   **You don't necessarily need to print your own copy of the feedback.** If you make sure that you save your feedback (and keep a backup copy), you can use your computer if you need to view your comments. You can always print out your copy at a later date, if you need to.

6   **Feedback could be provided in the form of a computer file.** If your trainees have easy access to computers, you needn't print their feedback at all. You could give them a disk with their feedback on it and they could read it on a computer.

7   **Feedback could be sent by e-mail.** This could mean that trainees could receive feedback from you very quickly.

8   **A spreadsheet can be used to provide quantitative feedback.** Spreadsheets have very good facilities for providing information such as averages and standard deviations. They can also quickly sort data into different orders. These facilities can be useful for feedback on some tasks, and they can also help trainees see how their progress relates to that of others in their group.

9   **You can't write on trainees' work by using a computer.** This can be a problem if you want to provide guidance for trainees. One way around the problem is for the trainees to number the paragraphs of their written work so that you can refer to these numbers in your feedback: for example, 'In paragraph 3.1 you stated that…'

10 **You can comment on trainees' work if it is a computer file.** If you are given work in the form of a document that you can load into your computer and edit, then commenting is relatively easy. You will need to make a clear difference between your comments and the trainee's work: perhaps you could put your comments in italics.

11 **You could add comments by using text boxes.** Many computer applications have a facility for adding text in boxes. You could use these for commenting on the work of trainees, and you could even use arrows to show exactly what you are commenting on.

46

Finding out how computer-assisted training is going

The danger is that only the *computer* knows how well trainees are learning things from it during computer-assisted training! The following suggestions may help you to keep track of your trainees' learning, and help you to focus your interventions.

1   **Watch carefully as trainees start working through any new computer-assisted program.** Whenever you notice anyone who has become stuck, or who looks puzzled, find out exactly what the stumbling block was. Sometimes, you may *intend* them to become momentarily stuck, so that they work out for themselves what to do next, but at other times you may wish to adjust your briefing instructions, or the program itself, to prevent them getting stuck at such points.

2   **Use any tracking capability already built into the computer programs.** Many computer-aided training packages automatically track the various pathways chosen by individual users, and it can be very worthwhile to retrack individual trainee's steps from time to time, to diagnose any aspects of the program which could be causing confusion.

3   **Ask your trainees what they think of the computer-assisted packages.** However, don't just ask general questions; structure your questions to focus in on particular aspects of the packages. In particular, if you already know that a given element of the package seems to cause problems, target such elements directly in your questions.

4   **Ask trainees what they like most about the training package.** It is useful to ask them for a given number of favourite things, two or three, for example. Analyze their responses, and look for ways that you can make more use of the things that they like. When selecting new packages, keep their preferences firmly in mind.

5   **Ask directly about what they *don't* like about the package.** Sometimes there will be nothing you can do to change the package itself, but you may still be able to adjust your briefings to trainees about how best to approach using the package. When possible, however, try to adjust the software itself so that the most common grumbles are eliminated.

6   **Consider getting the computer to collect trainees' feedback for you.** It may be possible, for example, to build into the training package intermittent multiple-choice questions about how trainees are feeling about the package at given stages, and to use the computer both to store their selections of options, and to give them feedback messages about the feelings they register.

7   **Sometimes, use *groups* of trainees to provide you with feedback.** The feedback that you can get from groups can be more valuable than from individuals, as you capture the products of group discussion. For example, ask groups to prioritize what they like best about the package, and what they like least.

8   **Use questionnaires carefully.** When people get too many questionnaires to fill in, they can become conditioned to respond to them at a surface level rather than thinking seriously about each question. Make question-naires really short and focused, and use them to target particular aspects of feedback that you are seeking.

9   **Don't ask questions lightly.** However trainees' feedback is being gathered, don't waste their time on questions where you don't want to (or don't need to) know the answers. For example, there's no point in gathering information on people's age, gender, occupation and so on unless you *know* that you intend to put to use the information that you gather. Most questionnaires can be reduced significantly without affecting their purpose.

10   **Give trainees feedback about their feedback!** If you're just seen to be gathering information rather than doing positive things *with* the data you collect, trainees may not be particularly willing to give you well thought out feedback. Show your trainees that you take their feedback seriously. Tell them what you are planning to do as a result of their feedback.

Conclusions

In a book of this scale, it would be futile to hope to cover everything that is important in the application of computers and communications technologies to training. The sophistication and power of the technologies are changing by the minute, and everyone involved in using such technologies continues to ascend a steep learning curve, with little sign of it levelling off. Perhaps the most significant danger is that, as trainers, we can be seduced by particular aspects of technology and forget the most important aspect of our work: the quality and scope of our trainees' learning. We hope that in this book we have kept the learning side of the training–learning equation at the forefront, and that our suggestions will continue to apply to the implementation and design of good quality training as the technologies continue to develop, both in sophistication and range. Technology changes fast, but human beings continue to learn in well documented ways, principally from learning-by-doing and getting feedback. The technologies that help either or both of these processes to occur successfully will be the ones that will prove most enduring in supporting effective training.

We will welcome your feedback on our suggestions in this book, and will be delighted to receive (care of our publisher) your own suggestions for future editions of this book. Meanwhile, we hope that you have been able to draw from this book, or extend from our suggestions, ideas that you can put into practice straightaway in your everyday work, and that can inform the development of your training to embrace the potential benefits that technology can bring both to you yourself, and to your trainees.

Tips on further reading

In line with the style of this book, here are some suggestions you should bear in mind before choosing where to look for one or more books to give you further help, both in developing your training techniques, and working out how best to use computers and communications technologies to support your training.

1   **If you're choosing a book on computers, make sure that the book is written for the computer system you are using.** For example, there are separate books on the same word processing packages or presentation managers, written for the Macintosh and for the PC. If you buy the wrong one, some of its contents may not apply to your system.

2   **Choose training books that fit the type of training you do.** If you can find plenty of useful food for thought in a few minutes scanning a book on training, it may be better than one where you have to search hard for anything you can put into practice straightaway.

3   **Make sure that a book about a particular software application is written for the correct version of the software you want to learn about.** For example, if you are using 'Word 97', don't be tempted to buy a reduced price book on 'Word 6' as the product has changed since the older book was written.

4   **Browse through any book to make sure that it is at the correct level for you.** You should look for a book that starts with introductory material that you may already be familiar with, but it must contain material that will advance your knowledge.

5   **Test the book's index.** Go to the bookshop or library armed with some questions that you need answers to. Does the book's index help you to find the answers easily?

6   **Don't be put off by patronizing books.** There are several series of books (such as the 'Idiots' or the 'Dummies' books) that you may find rather insulting in tone. If they contain the material you need, they can still be very useful.

7   **Some books include disks or CD-ROMs.** This can make the books seem very expensive. If the extra material on the disk or CD-ROM is good, it is good value for money, but sometimes this material is very poor quality. It will be difficult to evaluate it, but check the book to see what the content is.

8   **Look for reviews of books you might wish to buy.** You can often tell a lot about a book from published reviews in magazines and journals, especially if you already know and trust the opinions of a reviewer.

9   **If you like a book, look for others in the same series.** You will be used to the style and layout, so learning will be easier.

10 **Remember, any source is only a starting point.** Whether your aim is to become better at using computers to support your training, or at training about computers, your *real* learning happens when you try things out, and learn from triumphs and disasters alike. Books and other sources of information can give you ideas, and spare you from some of the disasters, but there is no substitute for having a go and seeing what works, and what doesn't work for you.

Other books on computing and training

The titles below represent a very small sample of the range of computing and training books available. If the topic you want isn't covered here, a good bookshop will probably have several books you could choose from.

Aitken, P (1994) *Idiot's Guide to 123 for Windows*, QUE, Indianapolis, USA.
This book is on a current version of Lotus 123, one of the very first spreadsheet programs. This series of books covers a wide range of topics in a very idiosyncratic style. You may find it patronizing, but the material is good.

Bourner, T, Martin, V and Race, P (1993) *Workshops that Work*, McGraw-Hill, Maidenhead, UK.
This is a collection of practical suggestions for making interactive training workshops effective and enjoyable, both for trainers and trainees.

Byrne, J (1995) *Easy Access for Windows 95*, QUE, Indianapolis, USA.
This is a good, clear introduction to Access, the database part of the Microsoft Office suite. There are several other computing titles in this series.

Cassel, P (1995) *Teach Yourself Access 95*, SAMS, Indianapolis, USA.
This is another book on Access, from another series of computing titles.

Courter, G and Marquis, A (1997) *MS Office 97 (No Experience Required)*, Sybex, California, USA.
An introduction to all the main components of MS Office, designed for beginners.

Cox, J and Dudley, N (1997) *Quick Course in Access 97*, Online Press, Washington, USA.
This covers the basics of using this database and, unlike the other weighty tomes listed here, is reassuringly thin.

Daniel, J S (1996) *Mega-Universities and Knowledge Media: Technology Strategies for Higher Education*, Kogan Page, London.
This book looks ahead to the way that information and communications technologies are likely to govern the shape of higher education in the next century. Many dimensions apply to the development of training in general.

Gertler, N (1997) *Using MS PowerPoint 97*, QUE, Indianapolis, USA.
This book gives clear tuition in PowerPoint, with a good glossary.

Greer, T (1998) *Understanding Intranets*, Microsoft Press, Washington, USA.
Loads of material to help you understand intranets, but you will need help
from your network manager to put it into practice.

Kennedy, J (1995) *UK Comms Information Superhighway*, BSB, St Albans, UK.
This book gives a very clear introduction to many aspects of data communications, including the Internet.

Kent, P (1994) *Complete Idiot's Guide to the Internet*, QUE, Indianapolis, USA.
This is a book, from another series, which gives a simple introduction to the
Internet. Again, its tone is a little insulting.

Levine, J *et al* (1997) *The Internet For Dummies*, IDG Books, Foster City,
    California, USA.
A cheap and cheerful introduction.

Levitus, B (1994) *Macintosh System 7.5 for Dummies*, IDG Books, Foster City,
    California, USA.
The 'Dummies' series gives clear help in using a range of computer packages.
This one is helpful for people who are learning to use Macintosh computers.

Mansfield, R (1997) *Excel 97 for Busy People*, Osborne/McGraw-Hill,
    California, USA.
Clearly set out and helpful, but very American.

McConnell, D (1994) *Implementing Computer-Supported Cooperative Learning*,
    Kogan Page, London.
This book gives much more detail than the present book on getting trainees or
students to work together, using computers and communications technologies.

McKelvy, M (1995) *Using Visual Basic 4*, QUE, Indianapolis, USA.
Visual Basic is a package for writing programs, so if you want to learn how to
do it, this book could help. There are other computing books in this series, too.

Mueller, S (1995) *Upgrading and Repairing PCs*, QUE, Indianapolis, USA.
There is a great deal of useful information in here if you have an old PC that
you want to keep going a bit longer.

Nadler, B (1994) *Computing for Cheapskates*, Ziff-Davis Press, Emeryville,
    California, USA.
Need we say more? There are plenty of hints here on saving money!

Navarro, A and Khan, T (1998) *Effective Web Page Design*, Sybex, California, USA.
This will help you design good Web pages, and comes with a CD of utilities and the code for all the pages discussed in the book.

Nelson, S (1995) *Field Guide to PCs*, Microsoft Press, Washington, DC, USA.
If you want to know more about your PC and how it works, this is a useful book.

Perry, G (1997) *Teach Yourself Windows 95 in 24 Hours*, SAMS, Indianapolis, USA.
This doesn't require you to work all day and night: it gives you 24 lessons, each about 1 hour long!

Race, P and Smith, B (1995) *500 Tips for Trainers*, Kogan Page, London.
This book is aimed at people who plan and run training workshops. This includes practical suggestions about many aspects of training, and should complement the present book well.

Race, P and McDowell, S (1996) *500 Computing Tips for Teachers and Lecturers*, Kogan Page, London.
Written in a similar style to the present book, this volume introduces various aspects of computers, printers and technology starting from scratch, and also gives some additional advice about getting people to learn from computers. It contains a glossary of some of the most common computer terminology.

Race, P and Brown, S (1998) *The Lecturer's Toolkit*, Kogan Page, London.
This photocopiable resource is A4 ring-bound, and can be ordered direct from the publisher. It contains detailed suggestions for lecturers, aiming to help them make their lectures, tutorials and assessments better learning experience for their students. Many of the principles extend to developing effective training programmes.

Wempen, F (1997) *Learn Word 97 In A Weekend*, Prima, California, USA.
An ideal book if you have to learn to word process in a hurry.

Index